£2   5/24

Deeper Sport Diving and Dive Computers

By
Steven M. Barsky

GW00708282

SCUBA DIVING
INTERNATIONAL

Deeper Sport Diving and Dive Computers
by Steven M. Barsky

Scuba Diving International
18 Elm Street
Topsham, ME 04086
Tel: 207-729-4201
FAX: 207-729-4453

Find us on the World Wide Web at http://www.tdisdi.com/

Photography
Principal photography by Bret Gilliam. ©Bret Gilliam. All rights reserved. Additional photography by Steven M. Barsky and Wayne Hasson.

Primary photo models: Lynn Hendrickson, Cathryn Castle, Lina Hitchcock, Gretchen Gilliam, Tom Burgener, Sarah Humphries, Brian Stephensen, Kristine Barsky, Don Santee, Dick Long, and Scott Lockwood.

Illustrations:
© Steven M. Barsky. All rights reserved.

Printed by Ojai Printing, Ojai, CA

ISBN Number:1-931451-03-6

Library of Congress Control Number: 2001093189

Other Titles Available from Scuba Diving International

Training Manual for Scuba Diving: Dive Training for the 21st Century
Easy Nitrox Diving
Night Diving, Underwater Navigation, and Limited Visibility Diving Techniques
Wreck Diving and Boat Diving Techniques
Rescue Diving Manual: A Guide to Rescue Techniques, Stress, Injury, and Accident Management
Dry Suit Diving
Solo Diving Techniques: A Manual for Independent Diving Skills
Visual Inspection Procedures: A Manual for Cylinder Safety
CPROX: Guidelines for Essential CPR and Oxygen Administration
CPR-FIRST: A Concise Manual for Emergency First Aid and CPR

Other Titles Available from Technical Diving International

Nitrox Diver Manual
Advanced Nitrox Diver Manual
Decompression Procedures
Semi-Closed Circuit Rebreather Manual: Draeger Units
Trimix Diving Manual
Extended Range Diver Manual
Cave and Cavern Diving Manual
Advanced Wreck Diving
Deep Diving: An Advanced Guide to Physiology, Procedures, and Systems
Nitrox Blending Manual: Guide to Preparation of Oxygen Enriched Air
Advanced Gas Blending Manual: Nitrox, Trimix, and Custom Mixes

WARNING!

Deep diving exposes the diver to certain risks that are unique to this type of diving. On deep dives, the diver will consume his breathing gas at a faster rate, and has less time to spend at depth before decompression stops become a necessity.

Improperly executed deep dives expose the diver to greater risks of out-of-air emergencies, hypothermia, nitrogen narcosis, and decompression sickness. Out-of-air emergencies during any dive can lead to drowning and lung over-pressure injuries, but on a deep dive they greatly increase the diver's chances of suffering from decompression sickness if the diver is forced to make a rapid ascent.

Hypothermia can lead to the inability to function properly during the dive causing drowning and can also increase the chances of decompression sickness. Nitrogen narcosis can decrease the diver's ability to function properly at depth leading to drowning, out-of-air emergencies, and inceased susceptibility to decompression sickness.

Decompression sickness can have both short term and permanent effects. These effects include, but are not limited to, loss of balance, loss of speech or hearing, paralysis, numbness, loss of bladder or bowel control, loss of sexual function, and difficulty in breathing. In severe cases of decompression sickness, death has resulted.

Even a properly executed deep dive can have unexpected consequences and there is always the chance that events beyond your control can lead to injuries or death when you are in the water. All diving presents some risk.

Dive computers have given divers tremendous freedom in making deep and repetitive dives, but like all electro-mechanical devices, they can fail unexpectedly. Even with proper use and without computer failure, there is still the small but real chance that you can suffer decompression sickness while using a dive computer. The same risks apply when using decompression tables or other decompression calculators.

This book has been written and designed to provide supplementary information for a course on deep diving using dive computers. It cannot provide sufficient information or experience by itself to enable you to participate in deep diving. Only through the use of proper equipment that has been maintained correctly, with training under the guidance of a qualified instructor, and continued practice, can you effectively participate in deep diving.

Table of Contents

Table of Contents

Table of Contents

Foreword by Bret Gilliam
President and CEO
Scuba Diving International

This text was designed to introduce you to deeper diving with the tools of a modern diver. It's the first of its kind to integrate computer theory into a deep diving course. That should be no surprise since SDI was the first international training agency to require dive computers as part of entry-level training. Now computers will help you venture past the first two atmospheres of depth and let you peek beyond the shallows into the blue.

How deep is deep? That's a question that historically has been difficult to answer within the diving community since so many factions have different perspectives. For instance, most technical divers consider "deep" to begin at 130 feet (40 metres), while commercial divers have successfully worked down to actual depths approaching 2000 feet of depth (610 metres).

Within traditional sport diving, deep has come to be defined as the zone between 60 (18 m) and 130 feet (40 m). On your first introduction to these depths, you probably will find that "deep" more than adequately describes your marine environment. When you consider that when you're 130 feet (40 metres) down underwater it's equivalent to looking back up at a thirteen story building... yeah, that's deep!

The great majority of diving done by sport divers all over the world is within this zone. And it is a fascinating world of marine life, shipwrecks, drop-off walls, exotic fishes, and colorful corals of impossible beauty. Indeed, you could spend the rest of your career as a sport diver and never run out of things to see and explore within these depths.

Technology has also made it easier and safer for divers to venture into the deep. Advances in regulator design let us breathe with less effort. Buoyancy control devices are more streamlined and provide more lift to accommodate carrying bigger cylinders. Exposure suits provide more warmth and protection in colder waters, and a host of other innovative gear provide endless choices to aid our enjoyment and safety.

But the single most valuable piece of equipment to evolve over the last two decades has been the electronic dive computer. Gone are the days when dive planning was controlled by manipulation of complicated dive tables requiring constant reference to depth, bottom time, surface intervals, descent and ascent rates, etc. Information had to be recorded underwater and at the surface to be transcribed into a logbook. If you made one mistake, the whole day's dive profile and decompression status could be compromised.

Today's modern dive computer incorporates the functions of a watch, depth gauge, and dive tables into one compact instrument that records all functions automatically and accurately. Dive computers allow the diver to plan dives in advance or on the fly underwater. They supply state of the art decompression algorithms far superior to dive tables both in physiological science and practicality. Just as important, dive computers have largely eliminated human error in calculation and record keeping. Overall, the sport of diving has become much safer and a whole lot more fun since the first dive computer was introduced.

It's exciting to see the sport mature, and it's a privilege to be on the cutting edge of training technology. Our author, Steve Barsky, is an ideal choice to explain deeper diving with dive computers since he is both an active dive instructor and an ex-commercial diver. Steve has also written many of the manufacturer's manuals on a variety of equipment for divers. His expertise lends itself to concise articulate explanations of complex subjects.

You will find your introduction to deeper diving to be exciting, challenging, informative and fun. Your training will open new vistas previously unimaginable underwater.

Enjoy this book, and most of all, enjoy yourself in diving!

Bret Gilliam
President and CEO
SCUBA DIVING INTERNATIONAL

Acknowledgments

My first real experience with frequent deep diving took place when I worked as a dive guide for a summer at the Underwater Explorer's Club at Freeport in the Bahamas. I was fortunate to work with several other instructors who shared their tips and techniques with me. We had an ideal environment, i.e., warm water, a short boat run to the dive site, plenty of back-up gear, and a recompression chamber within a short distance of the dive site.

My deep diving experience continued when I became a commercial diver and had the opportunity to run and make deep mixed-gas dives. I also learned to operate a recompression chamber and treated many cases of decompression sickness. During the time I worked as a commercial diver I was also subjected to decompression sickness myself, a common occurrence among divers in this profession.

In diving, we all learn from the know-how of other divers because nobody can be familiar with everything about our sport. My thanks goes out to all of my friends with whom I have shared deep diving adventures, particularly my wife, Kristine, with whom I have made so many memorable dives.

In preparing this book I was dependent on the cooperation of many people who contributed their time, their expertise, and information to help me get the job done. I am especially appeciative of the following:

- Jens Rubschlager at Oceanic
- Harry Averill with Dive-Rite
- Wayne Hasson - Aggressor Fleet
- Jamie Spicer at Scubapro/Uwatec
- Jim Clymer at AquaLung/Seaquest
- Larry Elsevier at Cochran Consulting
- David Crockford at SDI/TDI HQ in England
- John Wall at The Dive Shop, Fairfax, Virginia
- Ron Grzelka and Rob Arnold at Atlanta Scuba and Swim Academy
- Lynn Hendrickson, Brian Carney, Sean Harrison, and Cliff Simoneau at TDI/SDI

I hope that you have many deep diving adventures as you explore the underwater world.

Steve Barsky
Santa Barbara, California

Chapter 1
Into the Blue Depths

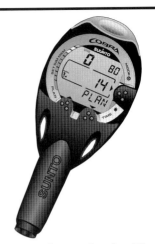

Sometimes, the best things to see underwater are at deeper depths. The coral "walls" of the Caribbean are a riot of color. The reefs that ring these islands rise vertically from the bottom out of thousands of feet of water, forming living "walls" of brilliant hues. As you drift over the edge of the wall, the water turns a darker, deeper mysterious blue, that looks almost purple. Open ocean fish, called "pelagics," swim along the face of the wall, giving you a glimpse of sharks, eagle rays, and other seldom seen creatures. Drifting along a vertical coral wall, with no bottom in sight, is very much like flying.

In the far Pacific, there is an island called "Chuuk" (formerly known as Truk), that was the site of a major battle during World War II. In 1944, American planes ambushed 50 Japanese ships that have remained on the bottom there since that time. Now, covered with soft corals, the slowly deteriorating remains of these wrecks lie at depths ranging from a few feet below the surface to over 200 feet (61 metres) down. Scattered along the decks and passages of these ships are dishes and cookware, lamps, navigation instruments, and even the skeletons of crew members. Many divers consider Chuuk to be one of the true "pinnacles" of the diving world.

There is something about deep diving that is irresistible to many people. There is an intensity to this type of diving that isn't found on shallower dives, where the light rays flicker over white sandy bottoms. As you look up at the hull of the boat, more than 100 feet (30 metres) above you, you get a perspective on your depth that can't be achieved in shallower water. Your regulator sounds different and the exhaust bubbles chime in tones that only a deep diver hears.

What is "deep diving?"

Divers have struggled to define deep diving for many years. Some people feel that any dive deeper than 60 feet (18 metres) is a deep dive, while others think that deep diving doesn't start until you are deeper than 100 feet (30 metres). A person who is engaged in "technical diving" may not consider a dive to be deep until it exceeds the generally accepted maximum limit for sport diving training of 130 feet of sea water (FSW). In the metric system this would be 40 metres of sea water (MSW). For a professional deep-sea diver, a dive might not be thought of as deep until the depth exceeds 200 FSW (61 MSW). As you can see, deep diving is a relative term, depending on the context of the specific diving situation to which it applies.

To understand the language of diving, it's important that we agree on some definitions before you read further in this book. Experts in diving generally agree on the following definitions:

• Recreational diving

Any diving done for fun. The diver is not being paid to go underwater. The exception are professional instructors who are paid to train other recreational divers.

• Sport diving

Diving done within the generally accepted depth limit of 130 FSW (feet of sea water) (40 MSW). This type of diving does not include diving that includes staged decompression or overhead environments, such as penetration wreck diving or cave diving.

• Technical diving

Diving that goes beyond the limits of sport diving, i.e., deeper than 130 FSW (40 MSW), or including staged decompression, or overhead environments. Technical diving is done for recreational purposes and the diver is not paid for his time underwater.

• Commercial diving

Any diving where the diver is paid to go underwater to perform heavy work. This may include the repair of underwater structure, such as bridges, the installation of pipelines, the salvage of vessels for profit, or other jobs.

Most deep diving for recreational purposes is done using ordinary compressed air or "nitrox," a special mixture of nitrogen and oxygen which contains more oxygen than ordinary compressed air. Even technical divers use

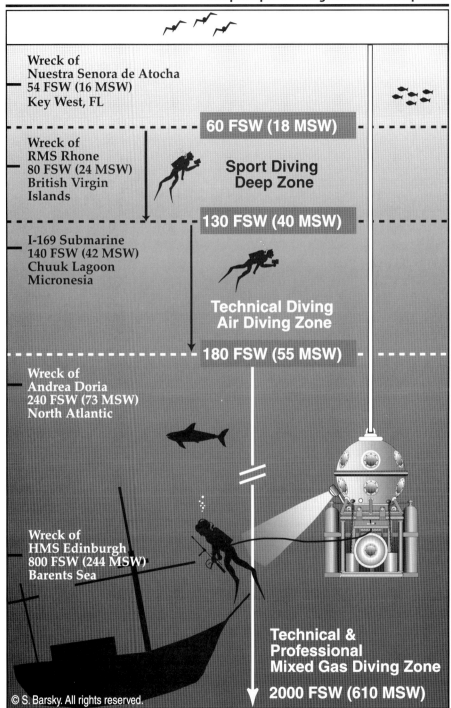

Wreck of
Nuestra Senora de Atocha
54 FSW (16 MSW)
Key West, FL

60 FSW (18 MSW)

Wreck of
RMS Rhone
80 FSW (24 MSW)
British Virgin
Islands

**Sport Diving
Deep Zone**

130 FSW (40 MSW)

I-169 Submarine
140 FSW (42 MSW)
Chuuk Lagoon
Micronesia

**Technical Diving
Air Diving Zone**

180 FSW (55 MSW)

Wreck of
Andrea Doria
240 FSW (73 MSW)
North Atlantic

Wreck of
HMS Edinburgh
800 FSW (244 MSW)
Barents Sea

**Technical &
Professional
Mixed Gas Diving Zone**

2000 FSW (610 MSW)

Depth ranges for different types of diving vary greatly.

Commercial divers use diving bells, fiberglass helmets, and hot water suits to make deep dives to 2000 FSW (610 MSW). As a commercial diver, the author, Steve Barsky, made working dives to 580 FSW.

compressed air for depths down to 180 FSW (55 MSW). However, starting at depths below 180 FSW (55 MSW) divers will use other gas mixtures, with the most common either being "heli-ox," containing helium and oxygen or "trimix," containing helium, nitrogen, and oxygen. Commercial divers have used helium-oxygen mixtures at depths down to 2000 FSW (610 MSW). This type of diving, commonly referred to as "mixed gas diving," is beyond the scope of this course, but you will hear divers use the term when they are discussing deep diving. Technical Diving International, the sister company to Scuba Diving International, offers courses in mixed gas diving.

For the purposes of your training with Scuba Diving International, we'll consider deep diving to be any dives conducted at depths in excess of 60 FSW (18 MSW). The maximum depth that you'll dive to during this training course is 130 FSW (40 MSW).

Why do people engage in deep diving?

As we've already discussed, there are many reasons to dive deep. You may want to see a particular reef or to photograph a special wreck. A marine biologist may want to dive deep to observe a particularly rare species of fish, while a cave diver may want to explore a previously unknown cave.

Deep diving by itself has no purpose. Divers use deep diving skills to take them to unique and unusual dive sites, and experiences that they cannot accomplish in shallower waters.

Some divers are under the mistaken impression that by participating in deep diving they will "prove" themselves and their capabilities. Nothing could be further from the truth. If you are considering participating in deep diving to feed your ego, you should look for another activity. Reckless deep diving endangers yourself, your dive partner, and other divers who may need to come to your rescue in the event that something goes wrong during your dive. You must have the proper "mind-set" to participate in deep diving.

How have dive computers changed deep diving?

In the early days of sport diving, divers who wanted to participate in deep diving had to plan their dives and execute them using the U.S. or British Navy Dive Tables. These tables were based upon mathematical formulas and experimentation in repetitive diving situations.

The tables were very restrictive, penalizing the diver for brief excursions to deeper depths, even if the bulk of the dive was conducted at a shallower depth. There were no provisions for divers who made these "multi-level dives."

With the invention of the first electronic multi-level dive computers back in the 1980s, divers gained great freedom. Not only did multi-level diving become practical, but if a diver accidentally exceeded his maximum planned depth, or stayed down longer than originally planned, the computer

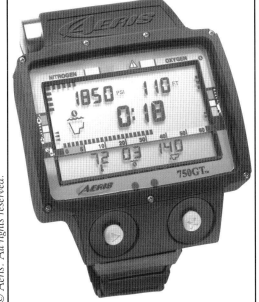

Dive computers have totally changed diving in the last 20 years.

would automatically calculate the new "dive profile." Dive computers also don't forget to include a dive time or a surface interval when making their calculations, and they don't make arithmetic mistakes.

Dive computers make it easy to plan your dives and quickly run different profiles to see the effect of changing variables such as the length of your surface interval. Air integrated computers also track your air consumption rate, which will help you in planning your breathing gas needs on future dives.

What will you learn during this course?

During this course you will work with your instructor to plan and execute deep dives down to depths of 130 FSW (40 MSW) using compressed air. In your dive planning you will use your dive computer plus information about the dive site, local facilities, and emergency procedures for your locale.

You will also learn to conduct simulated decompression dives, but no actual decompression dives will be made in this SDI course. Decompression diving requires additional equipment and training beyond the scope of this course.

You will use the skills that you learn during this SDI course as a foundation for further training in wreck diving, nitrox, and "extended range" or "technical diving." Deep diving requires more attention and planning than diving to shallower depths.

Scuba I.Q. Review

Talk with your instructor about your reasons for participating in deep diving and see if you can answer the following questions.

1) In recreational diving, at what depth do most people consider deep diving to begin?

2) What is considered to be the maximum depth limit for sport diving?

3) List three reasons why a person might want to participate in deep diving?

4) One major advantage of using a dive computer is that they allow you to make what type of dives?

5) How will an air integrated dive computer help you in planning future dives?

Notes

Chapter 2
How Deep Diving Affects Your Body and Mind

Deep diving has some interesting and important effects on both your mind and body. The main effect on your mind, nitrogen narcosis, is one you've already been introduced to in your initial scuba training. These effects are temporary, but can cause problems for some divers.

Deep diving can also be psychologically challenging for many divers, causing the diver increased stress. Recognizing this stress and dealing with it in appropriate ways is essential to your safety.

Your body has a number of different responses to deep diving. Depending on where you dive, the water can be much colder at depth, leading to a variety of problems if you aren't properly equipped. Nitrogen accumulation in the body increases with depth as well. Additional equipment can add weight that causes physical stress, especially on divers in poor physical condition.

Nitrogen narcosis

Nitrogen narcosis is a physiological condition that occurs when your nervous system is exposed to increased nitrogen pressure. While most textbooks will say that nitrogen narcosis occurs at depths of 100 feet (30 metres), some people begin to feel the effects of narcosis at shallower depths, while others aren't affected until much deeper.

Although we commonly hear about nitrogen narcosis, the more correct term would be "inert gas narcosis." An inert gas, like nitrogen, is any gas that does not chemically react in the body. Diving medicine researchers have found that any inert gas can produce narcosis, but the depth at which each gas begins to have an effect is different. "Lighter" gases, such as helium, do not begin to produce narcosis until the diver reaches great depths.

The exact mechanism by which nitrogen causes narcosis is not completely understood. Scientists believe that the source of the problem relates to the rate at which nitrogen dissolves into fatty tissues that cover the nerves in the brain. The nitrogen appears to interfere with the transfer of information from one nerve cell to the next.

Carbon dioxide, CO_2, which is the waste gas from our bodies, also seems to play a role in nitrogen narcosis. If you are working hard underwater, and not breathing deeply enough, a build-up of carbon dioxide in your body can make nitrogen narcosis worse.

Nitrogen narcosis produces a variety of symptoms including lightheadedness, a slowing of mental activity, problems with short-term memory, and a change in your sense of time. The symptoms tend to resemble drunkenness and make it difficult to perform simple tasks, such as properly reading and interpreting the data displayed by your dive computer. Obviously, none of these symptoms are desirable while you are underwater.

One of the more serious symptoms that may occur in divers who are affected by narcosis is a problem known as "perceptual narrowing." In this situation, the diver tends to focus down to a specific task, such as adjusting and aiming his camera, but fails to notice other events that are taking place around him underwater. When a crisis occurs during a dive, people who are suffering from perceptual narrowing may be completely oblivious to what's happening. This factor combined with the inability to perform fine motor skills – such as unclipping a small hook – can be disastrous in an emergency.

Many people feel that they are more affected by narcosis when they first reach the bottom, but with time, the narcosis is not as severe. There is no scientific data to back up this perception.

Many divers also report that they find that they develop a "resistance" or adaptation to nitrogen narcosis following repeated deep dives. Scientific tests

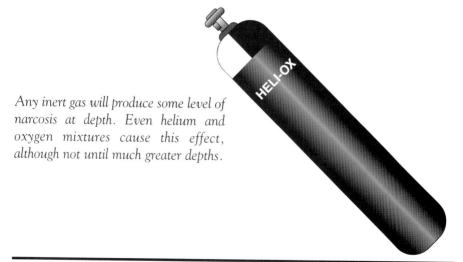

Any inert gas will produce some level of narcosis at depth. Even helium and oxygen mixtures cause this effect, although not until much greater depths.

Perceptual narrowing is not uncommon on deep dives. When this happens, the diver focuses in on one aspect of the dive and may fail to notice other things going on around them in the water.

Symptoms of Nitrogen Narcosis

Lightheadedness
Slowing of mental activity
Short-term memory problems
Perception of time affected
Perceptual narrowing

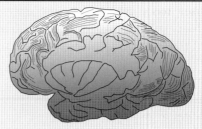

Nitrogen narcosis affects the brain in ways that are not completely understood.

that support this experience seem to agree, but there have not been enough controlled experiments to confirm this.

The symptoms of nitrogen narcosis disappear rapidly as you ascend to a shallower depth and there appear to be no lingering effects. During a dive if you feel uncomfortable due to narcosis, you should ascend to a depth shallower than 100 FSW (30 MSW).

Nitrogen absorption

Many divers confuse nitrogen narcosis and decompression sickness (DCS), probably because nitrogen plays a role in both situations. It is important for you as a diver to understand the difference between these two conditions. Nitrogen narcosis is all about short-term effects to your nervous system, but decompression sickness can have long-term effects on your body that can be extremely serious.

If you'll recall from your initial scuba training, air is a mixture of primarily nitrogen and oxygen. When you are on the surface, preparing to make your first dive of the day, the pressure of nitrogen inside your body is equal to the pressure of the nitrogen in the air surrounding your body.

Any time you dive underwater, as the pressure increases, your body absorbs more nitrogen. At depth, the pressure of nitrogen in your lungs is higher than the pressure of nitrogen in your blood stream, so each time you inhale through your regulator underwater, your body absorbs more nitrogen. In scientific terms, we say that the "driving pressure" of nitrogen is greater in your lungs and consequently more nitrogen diffuses into your blood stream. The tiny blood vessels, known as capillaries, that surround the "alveoli" (air sacs) in the lungs are where this gas exchange occurs.

As the nitrogen is carried throughout your body by the blood stream, it is absorbed by a variety of different tissues. For example, fatty tissues absorb nitrogen quite slowly and also release it slowly once it has been absorbed. We say that fatty tissue has poor blood circulation or that it is "poorly perfused."

Even though fatty tissue does not receive a high blood supply, the tissue itself has a capacity to absorb lots of nitrogen. When diving physiologists design and discuss decompression schedules, they consider fatty tissue as one of the "slow tissues" in regards to nitrogen absorption.

Other tissues, such as nerves, absorb nitrogen much more quickly. Nerves have lots of blood vessels to feed them oxygen and nutrients. Each different type of tissue has its own absorption rate. However, if you could stay underwater at one continuous depth for 24 hours, eventually, all of the tissues in your body would be completely "saturated" with nitrogen for that particular depth.

It takes time for your body to absorb nitrogen and time for your body to "off-gas," or release the nitrogen from your lungs. In reality, as a result of diving, we almost always have some bubble formation inside our bodies following a dive. These bubbles can be detected with the proper scientific instrumentation. Most of the time, these bubbles are small enough and occur in small enough quantities, that they do not cause a problem. Scientists sometimes refer to these bubbles as "silent bubbles" or "silent bends."

Once these bubbles in the body grow past a certain size, you will begin to experience the symptoms of decompression sickness. Any number of factors can contribute to causing decompression sickness including a lack of sleep, dehydration, and poor physical condition.

Under normal circumstances, if you follow the dive times and ascent rates allowed by your dive computer, you **probably** will never experience decompression sickness. Note that we say that you will probably never experience decompression sickness. The only way to be 100% certain of avoiding decompression sickness as a result of scuba diving is to never go underwater. When you dive, however, there is always some risk of decompression sickness, even if you use the tables or your dive computer perfectly. However, dive computers are far less likely to make a mistake in calculating repetitive dives and keeping track of depths and time than most people!

In reality, every dive is a "decompression dive," when viewed from the standpoint that when we descend to the bottom we place our bodies under pressure or "compression." When we return to the surface, we experience "decompression," as we reduce the pressure on our bodies. Although you may not be required to make formal "decompression stops" at the end of your dive, the slow ascent rate prescribed by your dive computer is a form of decompression. Of course, the smart diver always makes a "precautionary decompression stop," or "safety stop" at the end of each dive. However, just because you make a "safety stop" there is no guarantee that you will not suffer decompression sickness. A safety stop does not ensure your safety.

As a general result of decompression, and the flow of excess nitrogen in and out of our bodies, we experience a certain amount of physiological stress

Just because you make a safety stop there is no guarantee you will not suffer from decompression sickness.

during every dive. We feel this stress in the form of fatigue at the end of a diving day.

While a small amount of fatigue is recognized as normal, a diver who experiences weakness or exhaustion may be suffering from decompression sickness. Do not ignore these symptoms if they occur.

Decompression sickness can occur with divers who breathe other more "exotic" gases, such as helium and oxygen mixtures. However, the rate of saturation and desaturation of body tissues is different with each specific type of inert gas. There are special tables for diving with different gas mixtures, as well as special dive computers for these other mixtures.

Hypothermia

In most places in the world, the deeper you dive, the colder the water temperature will be. In some places, the difference between surface and bottom temperatures can be dramatic.

Cold water is another physiological "stressor," in that exposure to cold water makes your body take steps to help prevent heat loss. The body reacts by shutting down the blood vessels at the skin and redirecting the blood flow away from your arms and legs to help maintain the body's core temperature.

If the blood flow to the arms and legs was normal, the blood in the arms

Even in the tropics a wetsuit is usually a good idea. Although it's hard to believe, it's possible to suffer hypothermia in warm water.

and legs would cool and this colder blood would be carried back to your core, lowering your core temperature. By shutting down the flow to the arms and legs, your body attempts to preserve a normal core temperature. This increases the blood flow to the heart, making it work harder, contributing to your fatigue, especially at the end of the diving day.

Proper thermal insulation is important, even in tropical waters. Although many people wear dive "skins" in tropical waters, you'll probably find that a thin tropical wetsuit will be more comfortable in everything but the warmest waters.

During deep diving, if you use a wetsuit in colder waters, suit compression at depths of 100 feet (30 metres) or more is so great that the neoprene material has very little insulating capability left. This is one of the main reasons why most technical divers and serious deep divers use a dry suit for deep dives.

Heat loss also occurs due to the fact that you are breathing compressed air. Each time you inhale through your scuba regulator, the air expands as it flows from the tank through the first stage, and again from the second stage into your lungs. Each time the air expands, the pressure drops dramatically and the temperature decreases. Each breath that you take must be warmed up to your body temperature. Each time you exhale, you lose some body heat.

The deeper you dive, the denser the air you inhale with each breath, leading to further heat loss as the air molecules take on heat from your body and you exhale each breath. Respiratory heat loss increases as you descend. On deep commercial dives, professional divers use special breathing gas heaters to combat this heat loss.

When you lose too much heat from your body, there is a risk that you will suffer from "hypothermia." Hypothermia occurs when the diver's body core temperature drops below 98.6 degrees F (37 degrees C). Since water temperatures in most lakes and oceans are almost always colder than your core temperature, you will almost always lose body heat to the surrounding water.

The more time you spend underwater, the more heat you will lose. At some point in time, even relatively warm water will begin to feel cold to every diver. Some divers just take longer to chill than others depending upon their fitness level, percentage of body fat, activity level, and other factors.

Aside from the obvious discomfort of being cold, divers who become hypothermic also suffer from other effects including increased air consumption and impaired mental condition. A diver who is cold is also more susceptible to decompression sickness since the blood flow is restricted to the extremities. Decreased blood flow makes it difficult to eliminate nitrogen from your arms and legs.

Keeping your hands warm can be a critical issue on deep dives in cold water. If your hands get cold, you will lose your ability to manipulate fine controls, such as camera settings, or conduct other delicate tasks. If you wear thick mittens to keep your hands warm, this also can make it difficult to perform complex tasks.

When you combine the effects of cold and nitrogen narcosis on a deep dive, you can place yourself in danger. Wearing proper insulation is critical on deep dives.

Symptoms of Hypothermia

Increased air consumption
Loss of manual dexterity
Impaired mental capacity
Fatigue

It's essential to wear proper insulation, whether you are diving in cold water or the tropics. Gloves (or mittens), boots, and a hood are needed in cold water.

Fluid loss

Divers lose body fluids underwater through increased urine production and from the lungs. This can lead to dehydration and increased susceptibility to decompression sickness.

"Diuresis" is defined as an increased production of urine by the body. This occurs as part of the body's reaction to immersion in water that is colder than the body's core temperature. As blood is directed away from the skin, and a higher volume of blood circulates through the kidneys, urine production increases. This leads to a high volume of fluid loss. Each time you urinate underwater, you also lose body heat.

Fluid loss through the lungs occurs on every open circuit scuba dive. Scuba tanks are filled with air that has been filtered and dehumidified. As this dry air comes into contact with moist lung tissues, the air takes up moisture, and the net result is a high fluid loss with each exhalation.

Dehydration is a contributing factor in decompression sickness. When your body is circulating less blood, your gas exchange is not as efficient. In addition, as the blood thickens, bubble formation appears to be more likely. Blood flow is the most important factor in the exchange of dissolved nitrogen between blood and body tissues.

Dehydration also contributes to fatigue. When you have less blood volume your heart must work harder to circulate sufficient oxygen to all of the body's tissues.

Be sure to drink plenty of fluids between dives!

When dehydration occurs, you will notice a change in the color of your urine, which will become darker. Ideally, you should drink sufficient fluids to keep your urine clear, or at best, yellow. If you're not urinating (frequently), you're not drinking sufficient fluids! (If you are urinating frequently, you'll want to rinse your wetsuit out thoroughly after diving!)

You must make an extra effort to keep yourself well hydrated between dives, and especially when you are participating in deep diving. Fluid loss can be critical for the diver who is not careful about remaining well hydrated. Drink plenty of fluids, but avoid liquids that contain caffeine (such as coffee or tea) or alcohol, as these will contribute to further dehydration.

Physical stress imposed by diving equipment

Diving equipment itself imposes physical stress on your body every time you go underwater. The more equipment you wear, the greater the stress.

In warm, tropical waters, divers are usually not burdened with too much gear. In colder waters, however, the bulk, weight, and complexity of extra equipment can increase your physiological stress. The weight of extra equipment makes it more difficult to move around on deck, increasing your heart rate at the start of the dive. The bulk of extra equipment, and the drag it cre-

Diving equipment is heavy, and sometimes constricting, this causes your body to work harder.

ates in the water, will make it more difficult to swim, making you work harder underwater, increasing your air consumption.

While most regulators today provide excellent breathing characteristics, it's especially important to select a regulator that performs well if you plan on doing much deep diving. As your depth increases, the density of the gas you are breathing also increases. Poor quality regulators require you to exert more energy just to breathe this denser gas. For deep diving, be sure to select a high quality regulator that delivers air at high flow rates.

Psychological stress

Many divers are intimidated the first few times they make a deep dive. This is normal and healthy. Deep diving places you at a greater distance from the surface. There is less time to deal with anything that goes wrong because of limitations in your air supply and your no-decompression status. Prior to making a deep dive, almost all divers feel a certain amount of tension, whether it is their first deep dive, or they have made several prior deep dives.

Additional equipment used in deep diving can add to your "task loading," both in the preparation for the dive and the dive itself. The more equip-

It's not uncommon to feel apprehensive prior to a deep dive.

ment you carry and use, the more time it takes to set up and ensure that it is operating properly. Underwater, you are "tasked" with dealing with these items, in an environment where your performance will be somewhat degraded due to nitrogen narcosis. Until you are comfortable making deep dives, you should not carry additional accessories, such as cameras, that require you to divert your attention to dealing with the specifics of the operation of such specialized gear.

Anytime you have worries about making a dive, you should always stop to discuss them prior to descending, with your dive partner. In most cases, if you are feeling uncomfortable about making a particular dive, you may be surprised to find that your partner may be having some doubts, too, but was embarrassed to talk about it. It is considered perfectly acceptable to postpone or cancel any dive that you don't feel enthusiastic about making.

Divers who are distressed about making a deep dive are more prone to make mistakes underwater because they are concentrating on their fear, rather than enjoying the dive. In addition, if something goes wrong during the dive, they are more prone to make the wrong decision or panic when dealing with an emergency.

The best way to gain confidence in deep diving, or any diving activity, is to make progressively more challenging dives to build your abilities and self-assurance. In this course, you will make a series of dives, working into progressively deeper water, according to your skill and comfort level.

If you have enrolled in a deep diving course, but feel uncomfortable about making a particular dive, speak to your instructor and let him know about your concerns. It may be necessary for you to make additional dives to build your skills and reach a point where you are more relaxed in the water, before making deep dives. Everyone in diving progresses at a different rate, and you should never feel as though you must make a particular dive to keep up with your friends, spouse, or significant other.

Scuba I.Q. Review

Deep diving puts additional stress on both your mind and body. Review these factors with your instructor prior to your first deep dive.

1) Define the term "inert gas narcosis."

2) List three symptoms of nitrogen narcosis.

3) Define the term "decompression sickness."

4) Explain why every dive is a "decompression dive."

5) List three factors that contribute to fatigue following deep dives.

6) Explain why breathing compressed air underwater leads to body heat loss.

7) List two side effects of hypothermia that can cause problems for divers.

8) List two factors that cause fluid loss in divers.

9) Explain why caffeinated beverages and alcohol are not recommended between dives.

10) Explain how psychological stress can interfere with a diver's performance during a deep dive.

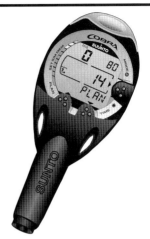

Chapter 3
Risks in Deep Diving

Smart divers recognize that deep diving poses some unique risks that must be kept in mind when planning and making these dives. Any time you add factors to a dive that make it more challenging, that require more equipment or additional training, there is additional risk. Deep sport diving is not considered a high-risk activity, but any diver should be able to appreciate the difference between making a dive on a shallow reef in 20 feet (6 MSW) of water and making a dive to 130 feet (40 MSW) along a coral drop-off. Deep diving is not a casual activity, but requires more planning and more precise execution.

In this chapter, we'll examine the special risks that are associated with deep diving, compared to the normal risks associated with all dives.

Nitrogen narcosis as a factor in diving accidents

Although it's difficult to confirm, nitrogen narcosis is probably a contributing factor in many deep diving accidents. When you aren't functioning at your full mental capacity underwater, the chances of an accident increase greatly.

One very common accident scenario, which has been repeated many times, is the diver who starts to make an ascent, but seems to be unaware that he is not rising off the bottom. This occurs for several reasons:

- The visibility is low and there are no visual cues such as kelp or a reef nearby to indicate the diver's position in the water.
- The diver failed to adjust for neutral buoyancy on the bottom.
- The diver fails to monitor his instruments to see if he was ascending.
- The diver is suffering from nitrogen narcosis.

Usually, the diver is just a few feet above the bottom and is kicking away, churning up a cloud of silt and thinking he is ascending towards the surface. At some point, the diver either runs out of air, or sinks back to the bottom and suddenly realizes he has not made any progress towards the surface. Without immediate positive action, an accident may occur.

It's also very easy for a diver suffering from narcosis to end up too deep when diving on a wall or wreck in deep water. This can lead to unplanned decompression or out-of-air emergencies.

The key to avoiding problems with nitrogen narcosis is to monitor yourself and your dive partner carefully on deep dives and to be aware when either of you is not functioning at full capacity. If you find yourself having difficulty controlling your dive, or you observe your partner having problems, you should ascend to a shallower depth as soon as possible.

If your dive partner exhibits odd behavior during a deep dive they may be suffering from nitrogen narcosis.

Rapid air consumption

You will find that your air consumption increases during deep dives for several reasons:

- The water tends to be colder, so your body "burns" more oxygen to stay warm.
- The pressure is greater, so you use more air each time you take a breath.

• Psychological stress causes most individuals to consume more air.

When you consume your air more rapidly, there is a greater risk that you will run out of breathing gas unexpectedly. As we'll see shortly, there is also a greater risk that you may suffer from decompression sickness due to greater nitrogen absorption whether rapid air consumption is due to cold, stress, and/or high workloads.

One of the most important steps that you can take to help prevent yourself from running out of air is to carry more air with you than you do on shallower dives. You can use a larger tank, double tanks, or carry a "bail-out bottle" (or pony bottle) with you as an emergency gas supply. How much air you need to carry with you will be determined by your personal air consumption needs.

Your air consumption will vary with a number of factors including:

• The water temperature and adequacy of the insulation you are wearing
• Your personal comfort level in the water
• Your personal level of physical fitness
• Your work rate during the dive
• The water depth

In tropical waters, most experienced divers find they can easily make a dive within the no-decompression limits to 130 FSW (40 MSW) and have sufficient air to make a precautionary decompression stop at 10-15 feet (3-5

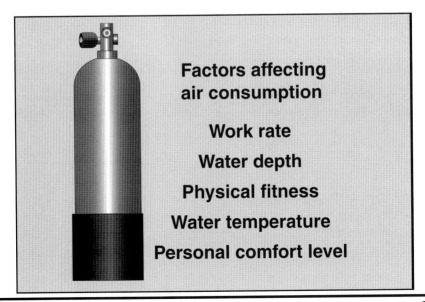

Factors affecting air consumption

Work rate
Water depth
Physical fitness
Water temperature
Personal comfort level

MSW) at the end of the dive and still surface with air in their tank. In colder waters, some people may not be able to do this.

Most sport divers today do not calculate their air consumption. They use a submersible pressure gauge and monitor their air supply. When they begin to run low on air they ascend.

By contrast, technical divers participating in deep dives (below 130 FSW or 40 MSW) need to know precisely how much air they will need to make the dive, as well as how much air they need to carry for decompression and contingencies. They use mathematical formulas in planning their breathing gas requirements.

The simplest way to deal with rapid air consumption at deeper depths is to carry more air with you. Of course, there is a trade-off between carrying enough air to meet your needs and carrying so much weight and bulk in air cylinders that you decrease your mobility on deck and underwater.

As you begin to participate in deeper dives, you need to develop an understanding and awareness of how much air you will need. We'll review your individual breathing gas needs in the Chapter 7 on Dive Planning.

Monitor your air supply carefully on deep dives.

Dangers of skip-breathing

One of the techniques that divers have used to try to extend their bottom time is to hold each breath for an extended period of time, rather than breathing in the preferred slow, deep rhythm used by experienced divers. This practice of holding each breath as long as possible is known as "skip-breathing."

Skip-breathing is a dangerous practice in any diving situation, but particularly during deep diving. When you engage in skip-breathing, you raise the level of carbon dioxide, CO_2, in your body. Carbon dioxide is the gas that triggers the urge to breathe in our bodies. As the carbon dioxide level increases, you feel a stronger need to breathe. A small amount of CO_2 is normal and natural in our bodies, but a large amount of CO_2 is dangerous.

Skip-breathing is a self-defeating practice because once the level of carbon dioxide begins to rise the urge to breathe increases. When the level of carbon dioxide in your body is raised, you will find it difficult to breathe for comfort if you must work hard during the course of the dive.

As we've already mentioned in the previous chapter, carbon dioxide also plays a role in causing nitrogen narcosis, so an elevated level of CO_2 is definitely undesirable during a deep dive. For these reasons, skip-breathing should be avoided during any deep dive.

Decompression sickness

Decompression sickness (abbreviated as "DCS") is one of the most serious risks in deep diving. While a "mild" case of decompression sickness may cause "pain only" symptoms, a serious case of decompression sickness can leave you paralyzed for life. Extreme cases of decompression sickness have caused death.

You may hear the term decompression sickness used interchangeably with the term, "the bends." For practical purposes, any diver would know that you were referring to the same thing, although medical personnel have more precise terminology that they may use. You may also hear some people refer to the term "DCI" or decompression illness, which is used to refer to both decompression sickness and the lung over-pressure accident that is known as an "arterial gas embolism" or "AGE."

Contributing factors in decompression sickness

There are many factors that can make it more likely that you will experience decompression sickness. The smart diver will attempt to minimize or eliminate as many factors as possible. Some of the known contributing issues that diving physiologists have identified include:

• **Age**
Older divers with poor circulation are more prone to decompression sickness and should be more cautious about deep diving.

• **Obesity**
Divers who are overweight have a greater likelihood of suffering decompression sickness because fatty tissue absorbs more nitrogen than lean muscle tissue.

• **Dehydration**
Whether due to alcoholic consumption (or other beverages such as coffee, tea, or caffeinated soft drinks) or warm weather, dehydration makes you more prone to decompression sickness.

• **Patent Foramen Ovale (also known as a "PFO")**
Prior to birth, when you were in your mother's womb, you were supplied with blood and oxygen from the umbilical cord that connected you to your mother's blood supply. During this time, there was a hole in your heart, known as a "foramen ovale," that allowed one side of your heart to communicate with the other. Once you were born, and the umbilical cord was severed, the foramen ovale should have closed, or at least it does in most children. Unfortunately, in about 30% of the population the foramen ovale does not close and remains "patent" or open, hence the term "PFO."

In divers, the PFO allows incomplete circulation of blood, where a portion of the blood bypasses the lungs, resulting in incomplete nitrogen elimination. Divers who have a PFO have a slightly increased risk of suffering from decompression sickness. After analyzing the statistics on diving accidents, diving physiologists have determined that due to the expense and difficulty of testing individuals for the presence of a PFO, it's not normally worth the risks involved. Divers are not routinely screened for this condition.

• **Cold**
Any time you are cold underwater, your circulation to your extremities will be reduced. This will make you more susceptible to decompression sickness. The instructions for most dive tables and the programs in many dive computers will take this factor into account in computing your allowable dive time.

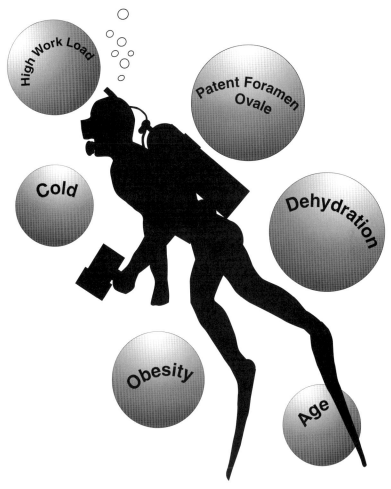

Many different factors may contribute to causing a case of decompression sickness.

• High Work Loads

If you are working hard, and breathing heavily, you will absorb more nitrogen than if you are relaxed and making an easy dive. Again, the instructions for most dive tables and the programs in many dive computers will take this factor into account in computing your allowable dive time.

Type I decompression sickness

Decompression sickness is normally classified by its severity. "Type I" decompression sickness is classified as "pain only" bends. In these types of cases, you might commonly experience pain in your shoulder, elbow, or knee. Other symptoms that also fall under the Type I category include skin rash or itching of the skin, and minor fatigue or loss of appetite. However, exhaustion is frequently a sign of the much more serious "Type II" decompression sickness.

Type II decompression sickness

"Type II" decompression sickness is considered severe, and includes any case that involves the nerves, breathing mechanism, and/or balance. Type II decompression sickness places you at extreme risk of permanent disability or death. Approximately 30% of all decompression sickness involves both Type I and Type II symptoms.

There are approximately double the number of Type II cases of decompression sickness compared to Type I cases, so the chance of you experiencing a serious case of decompression sickness is quite high. However, the overall incidence of all types of DCS is quite low. In fact, it has been determined that the incidence of DCS is probably less than 1% in the sport diving population.

The symptoms of Type II decompression sickness include the following:

- **Pulmonary Decompression Sickness**
(also known as the "chokes")
This occurs when inert gas bubbles block the artery that supplies the lungs. Fortunately, this is rare.

- **Neurologic Decompression Sickness**
Any case that involves the nerves is said to be neurologic decompression sickness. This is the type of decompression sickness that can leave you in a wheelchair for the rest of your life, with a complete loss of bowel and bladder control, and without sexual function. This also can include a loss of consciousness, memory impairment, visual disturbances, and changes in personality.

- **Vestibular Decompression Sickness**
(also known as the "staggers")
This occurs when delicate tissues in the middle ear that control balance are damaged as a result of inadequate decompression. The

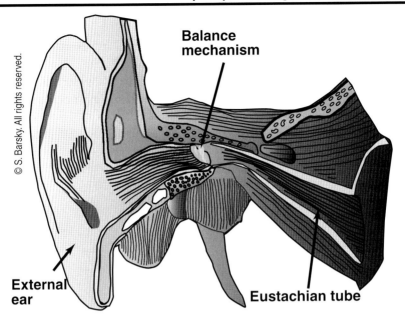

Balance mechanism

External ear

Eustachian tube

Vestibular decompression sickness, which affects your balance mechanism inside your ear, is extremely serious.

symptoms can include dizziness, nausea, vomiting, hearing loss, and ringing in the ears.

In a severe case of decompression sickness, you may experience any or all of the above symptoms. Obviously, these symptoms are frightening and cannot be ignored.

In some cases of decompression sickness, the symptoms appear within a few minutes of surfacing, but in many cases, the symptoms may not appear until hours after the last dive. No matter when the symptoms appear, it is essential to begin first aid and transport the victim to a hyperbaric facility as soon as possible.

Symptoms of Type I Decompression Sickness

Pain in joints
Itching of skin
Fatigue

Symptoms of Type II Decompression Sickness

Nausea	Dizziness
Paralysis	Convulsions
Ringing in ears	Personality changes
Visual disturbances	Difficulty in breathing
Loss of consciousness	Loss of bladder/bowel control

Denial

One of the biggest problems with decompression sickness is that many victims deny that they have a problem and postpone seeking treatment. There are many reasons for this, ranging from fear of looking foolish to the fear of interrupting a dive trip for the other members of the group.

No diver should ever feel embarrassed to report that they are experiencing symptoms of decompression sickness. Without prompt treatment, there is a strong risk that the damage from decompression sickness can be permanent.

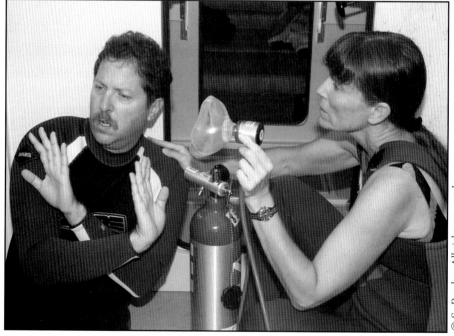

It's not uncommon for divers to try to deny they have decompression sickness.

The risk of decompression sickness is low

The risk of injury from decompression sickness in sport diving is real, but quite small. In a typical year, there are usually less than 500 cases of decompression sickness reported by sport divers in the U.S. When this figure is compared to the fact that there are over 2,300,000 active divers and the millions of dives that take place each year, you can see that your risk of suffering from decompression sickness is reasonably low, especially if you follow the precautions for safe recreational diving, i.e., practice good dive planning and observe recommended safety procedures.

Scuba I.Q. Review

Do you understand the risks in deep diving? Discuss these concepts with your instructor.

1) Describe two possible situations where nitrogen narcosis could lead to a diving accident.

2) List two factors in deep diving that could cause you to consume more air.

3) Define the term "skip-breathing" and explain why it is a bad practice for divers to follow.

4) List three factors that might contribute to causing you to suffer from decompression sickness.

5) Explain the difference between Type I and Type II decompression sickness.

6) Explain whether the risk of decompression sickness is high or low in sport diving.

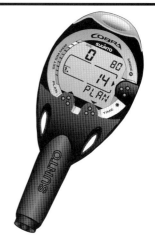

Chapter 4
Equipment for
Deep Diving

While it's possible to participate in deep diving without purchasing a great deal of extra equipment, you will find that your safety and enjoyment will be greatly increased with the addition of a few specialized pieces of gear. As in any diving, selecting the right piece of equipment can make a big difference in your experience.

Accessories for deep diving fall under two broad categories, "life support equipment," including tanks, bail-out systems, and similar items, and other simpler accessories, such as slates, decompression bars, and lines. You don't need to outfit yourself like a technical diver to participate in deep sport diving, but certain pieces of equipment will make it easier, safer, and more comfortable to conduct deep dives.

Life Support Equipment

Life support equipment is exactly what its name implies – i.e., any gear designed to help keep you alive in the underwater world. By this definition, a scuba regulator is life-support equipment because it provides you with air to breathe. Similarly, a dry suit is also considered life support equipment, because it keeps you warm and allows you to function in cold water.

The regulators available today deliver excellent breathing characteristics even during deep dives. We also have a wider selection of cylinders and better back-up equipment to make deep diving relatively easy and more fun.

Air cylinders

While the "standard" scuba cylinder found in most dive store rental inventories is the 80 cubic foot (10 litre) aluminum tank, there are many sizes and configurations of cylinders from which to choose. The aluminum 80 (10 litre) may be a good choice for routine sport dives, but there are other choices that may be more comfortable, and easier to handle, if you plan to regularly engage in deep diving.

For example, there are high-pressure steel cylinders that are quite compact and easier to carry than the aluminum 80 (10 litre). These high-pressure steel cylinders generally have more volume, a more compact size, and better buoyancy characteristics, too. For example, a high-pressure steel 100 cubic foot (12.2 litre) cylinder is roughly the same size as an aluminum 80 (10 litre) but holds 25% more air.

There are also low-pressure steel cylinders that may work better than a high-pressure aluminum tank. Generally speaking, steel cylinders have more favorable buoyancy characteristics than aluminum cylinders and do not experience a shift to positive buoyancy when they go from full to empty as aluminum cylinders. Most experienced divers tend to prefer steel cylinders over aluminum cylinders for these reasons.

Ideally, you want a cylinder that carries as much air as possible in the smallest possible size, with a low profile that sits close to your back. The fatter the cylinder, the further it will stick out from your back, throwing off your balance on deck and creating more drag underwater.

Sometimes, the best cylinder isn't a single large cylinder, but two smaller cylinders joined together by a "manifold." This type of arrangement may sit closer to your back than one large cylinder and may provide better balance.

If you are considering moving into "technical diving" in the future, a dual cylinder arrangement has certain advantages and may be a good choice for you. One of the biggest benefits of a dual cylinder arrangement is that the two cylinders can be joined by an "isolation manifold" that allows you to breathe off both cylinders at the same time, or isolate either one of the cylinders if necessary. There are also manifolds that will accept two regulators, so that an independent back-up regulator is always immediately available.

Whatever type of cylinder system you select, be sure that it is one that you can comfortably handle and is right for you. Smaller divers, who have smaller lung capacities, do not usually need to carry as much air as their larger dive partners. Your goal should be to always have more than "just enough" air available for the dive you plan to make.

Buddy independent alternate air source

Trying to share air with a dive partner on a deep dive can result in a dangerous situation, with two people fighting over one regulator. It is generally considered much safer if you carry your own true independent alternate air source. An independent alternate air source is generally defined as a separate

Relative Cylinder Sizes & Volumes listed by weight								
Imperial Version	Steel	Steel	Steel	Steel	Steel	Aluminum	Steel	Steel
Volume	125 cu. ft.	112 cu. ft.	98 cu. ft.	100 cu. ft.	85 cu. ft.	80 cu. ft.	80 cu. ft.	66 cu. ft.
Length	29"	26"	24"	25.2"	26"	27"	21"	21"
Diameter	8"	8"	8"	7.3"	7"	7.25"	7.3"	7"
Weight	45 lb.	41 lb.	38 lb.	36 lb.	31 lb.	31 lb.	31 lb.	25 lb.
Working Pressure	2640 p.s.i.	2640 p.s.i.	2640 p.s.i.	3500 p.s.i.	3500 p.s.i.	3000 p.s.i.	3500 p.s.i.	2640 p.s.i.
Buoyancy Full	-9.5 lb.	-8 lb.	-7.73 lb.	-11.5 lb.	-6.7 lb.	-1.4 lb.	-10.9 lb.	-5 lb.
Buoyancy Empty	neutral	-1 lb.	neutral	-5 lb.	neutral	+4.4 lb.	-4 lb.	-1.67 lb.

Scuba cylinders come in many different sizes and you should select the size that works best for you.

Relative Cylinder Sizes & Volumes listed by weight

Metric Version

	Steel	Steel	Aluminum	Steel	Steel	Steel	Steel	Steel
Volume	10 litres	10.4 litres	11 litres	12.2 litres	15.5 litres	15 litres	18 litres	20 litres
Length	53 cm.	53 cm.	68.6 cm.	17.8 cm.	64 cm.	61 cm.	66 cm.	73.6 cm.
Diameter	17.8 cm.	18.4 cm.	18.4 cm.	17.8 cm.	18.5 cm.	20.3 cm.	20.3 cm.	20.3 cm.
Weight	11.3 kg.	14 kg.	14 kg.	14 kg.	16.3 kg.	17.2 kg.	18.6 kg.	20.1 kg.
Working Pressure	172 bar	232 bar	207 bar	232 bar	232 bar	172 bar	172 bar	172 bar
Buoyancy Full	-2.3 kg.	-4.9 kg.	-.63 kg.	-3.03 kg.	-5.2 kg.	-3.5 kg.	-3.6 kg.	-4.3 kg.
Buoyancy Empty	-2.3 kg.	-1.8 kg.	-2.0 kg.	neutral	-2.3 kg.	neutral	-.45 kg.	neutral

Relative tank size and volumes in metric.

This diver is using two scuba cylinders joined together by an isolation manifold. The valve between the two cylinders allows either cylinder to be isolated from the other. Each cylinder has its own independent regulator. This arrangement provides the diver with many options in regards to how the air supply may be used and managed.

air cylinder with its own regulator system that is carried by the diver for use in emergencies.

If your deep diving system does not include dual air cylinders with a back-up regulator, it is strongly recommended that you carry some type of independent air source whenever you make a deep dive. There are two main configurations that are commonly used, the "pony" or "bail-out bottle," which includes a conventional scuba regulator, or the integrated system with a built-in regulator, like "Spare-Air®."

A "pony" bottle or "bail-out bottle" is a small scuba cylinder, usually 13 or 19 cubic feet (2-3 litre), with an ordinary scuba regulator attached to it. The cylinder is mounted on the side of your scuba tank where it is accessible if needed. The second stage from the regulator may be routed to the diver's chest and attached with a quick-release clip or a loop of stretchy surgical tubing.

There are a variety of mounting arrangements for bail-out bottles including metal clamps, Velcro® bands, and canvas bags. You should select whichever arrangement works the best for you with the other components of your diving system. Ideally, the bail-out should be set up so it creates as little drag as possible and is in the least likely position where it could cause entanglement.

While all bail-out regulators should be equipped with a submersible pressure gauge, it need not be the traditional large gauge mounted on the end of a high-pressure hose. Compact pressure gauges can be purchased which mount directly on the first stage, eliminating another hose and its bulk.

A pony bottle with an independent regulator provides a true alternate air source.

A *compact submersible pressure gauge like this one is perfect for use on a bail-out bottle.*

The advantage to a bail-out system is that it provides a large reserve air supply and the cylinder size can be changed according to your needs. The disadvantages of this type of arrangement are the expense, bulk, and weight of the gear.

Integrated alternate air supplies like Spare-Air® are also available. These systems use a compact regulator where both the first and second stage mount together directly on the cylinder. There is no low pressure hose connecting the first and second stage. This design results in an extremely compact unit that can be mounted almost anywhere you choose. The cylinder is normally carried in a holster that mounts on the diver's buoyancy compensator.

Systems like Spare Air® are typically less expensive than conventional bail-out bottles and extremely compact. Since the system is entirely self-contained and compact, it can be handed off to another diver in an emergency. The drawback to this type of system is that it does not provide as much air as

Compact, independent alternate air sources are convenient, but not all hold enough air.

a bail-out bottle and the cylinder size cannot be easily changed. Systems like these may not provide sufficient air for some divers at the deeper end of the sport diving range.

Buddy dependent alternate air sources

Dependent alternate air sources, such as octopus rigs, provide emergency air only for your diving partner, not for you, and only provided that there is sufficient air remaining in your tank for both of you. In addition, when two divers are breathing off the same first stage at depth, particularly when they are stressed, there is usually some decrease in regulator performance.

You can probably get by in most sport diving situations using a long hose octopus rig or a power inflator that doubles as an emergency-breathing regulator. These devices weigh less and create little additional drag when compared to a completely independent air supply. They are also easier to transport if you are traveling by air.

The long hose octopus provides the most distance between you and your dependent dive partner. This arrangement allows you to swim through dive locations where it may be difficult to maneuver while sharing air, such as wrecks or kelp forests, without the need to be face-to-face. While technical divers, such as cave divers, use hoses that may be as long as seven feet, for sport deep diving, you do not need a hose this long. A 42-48 inch (107-122 centimetres) long hose is usually sufficient for deep diving that does not involve penetration of wrecks or cave diving.

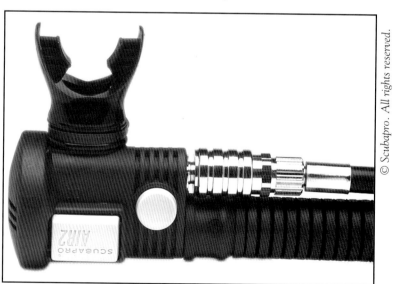

This combination power inflator/regulator is convenient to use.

You do not need an excessive amount of lift for deep diving in the sport diving range. Select a BC with sufficient lift for your personal needs.

Power inflators that have integrated second stages help to reduce the number of hoses in your diving system and simplify your gear. However, it's difficult to fit these systems with sufficiently long hoses to allow separation between you and your dive partner in a situation where you need to share air. These systems are best used when you as a donor switch to the power infla-tor/regulator and allow your partner to use your primary regulator. This situ-ation will place the two of you physically close and requires that each diver be well coordinated, as well as experienced.

Buoyancy compensators

If you decide to purchase a larger tank or twin cylinders, be sure to care-fully re-evaluate your buoyancy needs. Most larger cylinders are very nega-tively buoyant when full and some remain negatively buoyant even when empty. You must have sufficient buoyancy in reserve to make yourself posi-tively buoyant underwater when fully equipped.

The preferred buoyancy compensator is the one that gives you just enough buoyancy (lift) to support your head out of the water comfortably when your tanks are full and you have all the gear and accessories you will carry during the dive. Any additional buoyancy capability beyond that can create problems in terms of excess volume that must be vented and addi-tional drag due to bladder size.

Some technical divers carry so much weight in the cylinders that they use that they do not need to use a weight belt due to the negative buoyancy of their tanks. This should not be the case for anyone involved in sport diving.

Although many technical divers use dual bladder buoyancy compensators, they are considered unnecessary for sport diving. While dual bladders provide redundancy for technical dives, they add expense, complexity, and bulk that are considered undesirable for sport diving.

High performance regulators

Any regulator used for deep diving should have a sufficiently high flow rate that it is capable of providing air easily at a depth of 130 FSW (40 MSW), even if you are working hard. If you plan to use an octopus rig, then the regulator must be capable of supplying air for both divers.

The first stage of your regulator should be a "balanced design." This means that the regulator will breathe just as easily when the tank is full as when you are low on air. The first stage may be either a piston or diaphragm design, although piston regulators seem to have a slight edge in reliability due to the fact that they typically have fewer moving parts.

The second stage of your regulator should be matched to the first stage in terms of its performance capabilities. Some first stages deliver higher intermediate pressures than others and will not work properly with all second stages.

Be sure that any regulator that you select has an adequate number of low and high-pressure ports to accommodate your needs, now and in the future. For example, the regulator should have a minimum of three additional low-

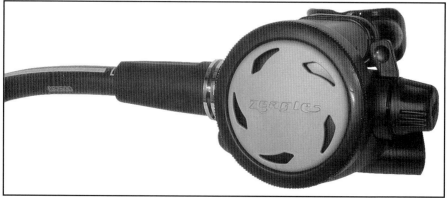

Your regulator should breathe comfortably at the depths where you plan to dive.

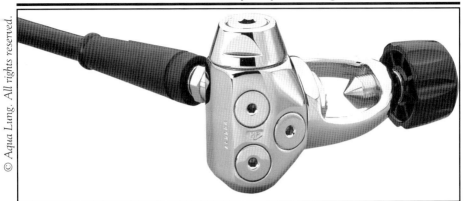

Your regulator should have a sufficient number of low pressure ports to accommodate any accessories you may need to add to it.

pressure ports to accommodate a dry suit inflator hose, an alternate air source, and a BC inflator mechanism. Extra ports are desirable so you can route the hoses where they need to go depending on the equipment that you are using. Similarly, a second high-pressure port will give you an option in deciding where to route your submersible pressure gauge.

Any top of the line regulator from a major manufacturer should be capable of providing sufficient air at depth. If you have any doubts about the regulator that you are currently using, be sure to check with your instructor.

Hang-off bottle and regulator

Another back-up system that may be used on a deep dive is a "hang-off bottle" with its own regulator (with at least two second stages) positioned at a depth of 15-20 feet (4.5-6 metres) below the boat. The purpose of this system is to supply air to any diver who may not have sufficient air to complete his precautionary decompression stop (safety stop). Or, in the event that you have accidentally exceeded your maximum depth or bottom time, to provide you with enough air to fulfill any actual decompression obligation you might incur.

The bottle must be turned on before the system is placed in the water or the first stage of the regulator will flood and need to be serviced. In most situations, the bottle is turned on and then turned off. If you find you need to use a bottle in this type of situation you must remember to turn the bottle on immediately as soon as you reach the cylinder. In some situations, if you want to leave the regulator on, you may prefer to "plug" the regulator using an accessory octopus regulator mouthpiece plug to prevent free-flow as the tank moves up and down in the water column.

For divers who are properly trained, the use of nitrox, gas mixtures containing more than 21% oxygen, or 100% oxygen, can greatly speed up nitrogen elimination and help increase your safety at your precautionary decompression stop following deep dives. Just as 100% oxygen helps to rapidly eliminate nitrogen from your system during treatment for decompression sickness, breathing nitrox or pure oxygen during decompression can help to prevent decompression sickness before it occurs.

Any hang-off system that uses more than 40% oxygen or pure oxygen must be specially prepared for this use. Preparation of this equipment includes proper cleaning, use of oxygen compatible seals and components, and use of oxygen compatible lubricants. Equipment that has not been properly cleaned and configured that is exposed to high-pressure oxygen can result in fires or explosions.

The use of nitrox can greatly speed up nitrogen elimination following deep dives.

Emergency oxygen should always be on hand for all diving activities

Oxygen systems

Oxygen should always be available for any organized dive, and especially for deep dives where there is greater risk than on shallow dives. There should be sufficient oxygen for at least one diver to breathe for the time it would take the boat to make it back to shore, or until the diver can be evacuated by helicopter.

If you are diving from a small boat, where it may be difficult to carry multiple oxygen cylinders, there are systems available that will allow you to extend the capability of your oxygen supply. These systems function in a fashion similar to a rebreather and allow you to more than double the capability of the oxygen you have on hand. The oxygen in the unit is recirculated and any carbon dioxide is "scrubbed" out of the breathing "loop" by a special chemical absorbent.

Although these oxygen-recirculating systems are simple to use, they require special training beyond what you would receive in an ordinary oxygen administration course. If you plan to dive from your own small boat and travel more than an hour from shore, you should consider carrying this type of system aboard your boat.

Thermal protection

For deep diving, it is essential to wear sufficient thermal protection to make the dive comfortably. Whether you are diving in the tropics or the north Atlantic, the right thermal protection is critical.

You should select whatever thermal protection is comfortable for you, regardless of what your dive partner selects. Smaller divers tend to need more thermal protection than larger divers due to their greater surface area relative to their body mass. Older divers may also find that they need more thermal protection to feel comfortable.

For diving in waters between 65 and 70 degrees F (18-21°C) a wetsuit that is 7 millimetres (or 1/4 inch) thick will provide adequate protection for most divers on a short duration deep dive. In waters above 70 degrees (21°C) but less than 80 degrees F (27°C), most divers will find a full 3-millimeter (or 3/16 inch) wetsuit will be adequate. At 80 degrees (27°C) and above, most people can get by with a shorty suit or a dive skin.

Proper thermal protection is especially important on deep dives.

Photo by S. Barsky © DUI

To get the most out of your dry suit, you need to wear proper insulation under it.

Photo by S. Barsky © DUI

A well-designed wetsuit will provide the maximum insulation for your torso, with less insulation on your arms and legs. Most divers find that a farmer john style pair of pants and a jacket with an attached hood work best. The farmer john and jacket keep your core warm while still providing the flexibility in your arms and legs for swimming and operating other equipment.

Proper insulation for your head, hands, and feet is also important. These are all high heat loss areas, due to their tremendous surface area. Heat loss from your head can be especially high, since the body cannot shunt blood away from your brain, but must keep it continuously oxygenated with a high blood flow. Whether you wear a wetsuit or a dry suit, a good pair of gloves, boots, and a hood are needed in cold water.

For water temperatures below 65 degrees F (18 C) a dry suit is usually recommended. There are many different types of dry suits, depending on the type of diving that you do. For example, if you plan to use your dry suit for wreck diving, a crushed neoprene suit would be a good choice, due to the abrasion resistance of this material. Conversely, if your primary objective is underwater photography, you may find that a more flexible suit, made from trilaminate material is a better choice.

No matter what type of dry suit you purchase, it won't perform well unless you invest in a good set of dry suit underwear. For extended dives in cold water, Thinsulate® is a good choice. Thinsulate® has the advantage that it provides good insulation even if the underwear becomes wet.

Polartec® is another synthetic fabric that provides good insulation and has excellent stretch. It is extremely comfortable to wear and easy to don. Your weight requirements with Polartec® will generally be low.

Proper thermal protection for a deep dive will not only help you to get the most out of your air supply, but will also help to protect you from decompression sickness.

Dive computer

The modern electronic dive computer has made deep diving much easier than it was in the past. By eliminating the need to make mathematical calculations and providing you with up to the minute data on your remaining allowable dive time as your depth changes, the dive computer gives you the freedom to explore the underwater world at will. We will discuss dive computers in detail in the next chapter.

Additional accessories

Dive Light

A dive light is an excellent accessory to carry on almost any deep dive. Without a dive light, even during the daytime, you will miss the fabulous colors to be seen on deep wrecks and coral walls.

There are many compact lights that put out a wide beam with plenty of power. Be sure to use a removable lanyard on your light so that you can disconnect the light from your body quickly in case it becomes entangled with lines or other items underwater.

A dive light will help you to see the colors at greater depths, even during the daytime.

Weight systems help to transfer the strain of your weights from your hips to your shoulders.

Weight systems

If you will be wearing a wetsuit or foam neoprene dry suit, keep in mind that you will have tremendous suit compression on a deep dive. An ordinary nylon weight belt will have a tendency to slide around on your waist, and the buckle could end up in back of you. In a worst-case situation, if you have slim hips, it's even possible for your weight belt to slide off. If you have a nylon belt, you'll need to check your belt and tighten it up as you descend.

If you do lots of deep diving, there are other alternatives to nylon belts, such as stretch belts and weight harnesses. Stretch belts may be made from solid rubber or may be rubber-impregnated fabric. These systems can be tightened up sufficiently prior to the dive so that they won't move around.

Special weighting systems are also available that consist of a shoulder harness with an attached belt. These systems stay in one place without moving and have the added benefit of transferring the weight to your shoulders, taking the strain off your hips and lower back.

Slates are for data

Plastic slates are handy for recording all types of information from your dive. If your hands are wet on deck, if you're in a small boat where nothing is dry, or if you need to write down information underwater, there's no substitute for a plastic slate.

Although most dive computers now have the capability to download information to a personal computer, not all do, so you may need a slate to copy and transfer information to your logbook. In addition, there is always information from your dive that your dive computer will not record, such as visibility, your diving activity, or details of the dive site.

Slates are also a simple means of communicating with your dive partner underwater. You can write messages to each other that are impossible to communicate through hand signals.

Hanging out at the "deco bar"

"Deco bar" is a short way of saying "decompression bar." A decompression bar is a bar hung from the stern of the dive boat to provide a stable platform for divers to use to hang onto to complete a precautionary decompression stop (safety stop) or actual decompression.

On most deep dives your ascent and descent will be made on the anchor line of the boat you used to travel on to the dive site. While the anchor line is a common place to make your descent and ascent, it's not usually a good place to make a safety stop. In any but the calmest conditions, the anchor

Slates are a useful way to communicate and record data.

The use of a deco bar makes safety stops more comfortable and easier to perform.

line on most boats heaves up and down several feet each time a wave passes under the boat. This makes it difficult or impossible to maintain a constant depth while making your safety stop. In addition, if there are several dive teams in the water at the same time, it is usually impossible for more than two or three divers to hang onto the anchor line at the same depth. If the anchor "line" is chain instead of rope, there is also the danger that you could be injured or the chain could damage your equipment as the line snaps up and down.

There are several reasons why the deco bar is hung at the rear (stern) of the boat, but the most important is that the stern of the boat typically is more stable and has less vertical movement than the front (bow) of the boat. By positioning the deco bar at the stern, it is much easier to stay at the same depth while making your stop. It is also easier to hang the bar from the two corners of the stern than along the side of the boat, and the bar is immediately adjacent to the ladder or swimstep at the stern.

The deco bar is also the location where the hang-off bottle will normally be positioned.

Using a reel to return to the anchor line

In low visibility, many divers use a reel to help them return to the anchor line. The free end of the line is connected to a piece of wreckage close to the anchor, using a snap hook for quick attachment, and the line can be paid out as you explore the wreck. Fastening the line to the anchor is not a good idea, in case the anchor drags or the boat needs to pull the "hook" in an emergency.

At the end of your dive it's easy to return to the anchor. You simply reel up the line and you're back at the anchor, ready to make your ascent.

Different types of reels have different features. Check with your instructor to see what types of reels are considered desirable in your area.

Using a lift bag, reel, and line for safety stops

A technique that is popular with wreck divers on the east coast of the U.S. is to use a "lift bag" with a line and reel for making decompression stops, rather than depending on using the hang-off bar (deco bar) to make their stop. Specially designed bags known as "decompression buoys" are also used.

A lift bag is a heavy-duty inflatable fabric bag that is usually open at the bottom end The bag is equipped with D-rings at the lower end to allow it to be fastened to heavy objects underwater for lifting. The bag is usually inflated using a spare regulator and tank.

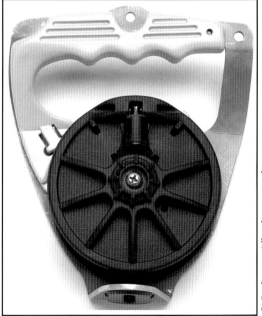

There are many different types of reels that can be used to help you return to the anchor line. Check with your instructor to see what kinds are used in your area.

Decompression buoys are similar to lift bags but are usually sealed and equipped with a special relief valve to vent excess pressure as the bag floats to the surface. Lettering on the bag identifies its purpose and the fact that there is a diver underneath it, to caution boat operators who may not be familiar with diving operations.

Divers may use a variety of reels underwater to assist them in making safety stops when the boat has pulled off site or if they were unable to return to the anchor underwater, if the boat has dragged anchor or the anchor line has been severed. In situations where there is no strong current, you fasten your line to the wreck and unreel it as you make your ascent to your safety stop. When you are at the appropriate depth for your stop, you inflate the lift bag to mark your position. Once you have completed your stop, you release the line, surface, deflate the bag, and signal the boat to pick you up.

Some divers use natural fiber rope, like manila, on large reels, working under the assumption it may not always be possible to recover a line that has been fastened to a wreck. Natural fiber ropes will disintegrate over time leaving no remains behind. If you use a natural fiber rope for this purpose it should be wetted down and stretched out before you wind it onto a reel. If you fail to wet the line before you use it in the water the line will constrict into a knotted mass that will be difficult or impossible to use.

Synthetic line such as braided nylon is typically used on smaller reels. Synthetic line has the advantage that it runs through fittings and restrictions

In some areas, decompression buoys are used by divers to provide a comfortable platform for performing safety stops or decompression.

This diver is using a reel with a natural fiber rope, known as "manila" to reel up from the wreck to perform his safety stop.

more easily, is usually lighter weight and has greater strength, and does not wear out quickly. If a synthetic rope is used, it is usually fastened through the wreck with a loop that can be released so the line can easily be recovered.

In cases where the boat has moved off site, and there is a heavy current, it may be more desirable to make your ascent to your safety stop without fastening off to the bottom. A strong current can make it extremely difficult to hang onto a line or maintain the proper depth for your safety stop. If there is a current, once you reach your stop, you inflate your lift bag, make yourself negatively buoyant, and "hang" from the buoy. This method requires excellent buoyancy control to avoid overshooting your safety stop if you make your ascent without being tethered to the bottom.

When the current is strong and you make a stop using this technique, you will be drifting away from the dive site. You must be equipped with signaling devices to gain the attention of the boat crew to avoid becoming lost at sea. Obviously, this technique is only for highly experienced divers.

There are several different methods of using a decompression buoy, reel, and line. Your instructor will show you how this is practiced in your local area.

Signaling devices

Since most deep dives are made from boats at distant offshore locations, it's important to carry at least one, if not more, signaling devices with you in case you are unable to swim back to the dive boat. The most commonly used devices are sound signaling devices and visual devices.

The simplest sound signaling device is a whistle, and these are effective provided you are not too distant from the dive boat. The most effective sound signaling devices are air powered horns that use compressed air from your buoyancy compensator and connect between the inflator hose and your BC.

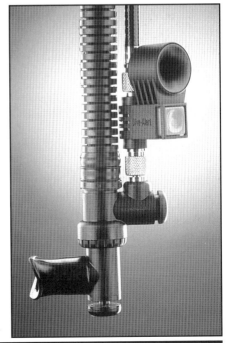

Air powered horns are the most effective sound signaling devices.

Flares are extremely effective visual signaling devices for both day and night use.

Visual devices include stainless steel mirrors, inflatable tubes, and flares. Obviously mirrors and inflatable tubes can only be easily seen during daylight hours, but flares can be seen both day and night. A flashlight or strobe can also be used for signaling at night.

EPIRBs (Emergency Position Indicating Radio Beacons) are electronic devices that are used to help find a "lost" diver on the surface. They are extremely effective in helping a boat to pinpoint a diver's exact location on the surface of the ocean.

Scuba I.Q. Review

Diving is an equipment dependent sport and you will want to have the proper equipment available for making deep dives. Review your equipment options with your instructor and discuss the following questions.

1) Describe other cylinder systems that may be preferable to an aluminum 80 cubic foot (10 litre) cylinder for deep diving.

2) List two types of buddy independent alternate air sources.

3) List the two types of buddy dependent alternate air sources.

4) State the amount of lift (buoyancy) required in a buoyancy compensator for deep diving.

5) State the minimum number of low-pressure ports your regulator should have and the accessories that might be connected to these ports.

6) Define the term "hang-off bottle."

7) Explain why nitrox or 100% oxygen are frequently used by divers at their safety stop following a deep dive.

8) State the water temperature below which a dry suit is usually recommended.

9) List two uses for a slate on a dive trip.

10) Define the term "deco bar" and explain how this device is used on a deep dive.

11) Explain how a decompression buoy is used at the conclusion of a dive.

12) List two possible uses for a reel and line on a deep dive.

13) List two types of visual signaling devices used by divers.

14) List two types of sound signaling devices used by divers.

Chapter 5
Understanding and
Selecting Dive Computers

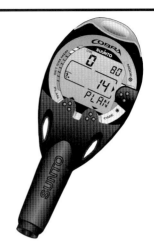

The introduction of the first successful electronic dive computer, the Orca Edge, in 1983 was a shattering technological change in sport diving. When they were first introduced to the market, many people thought that computers were "dangerous" and that people who used them were more likely to get "bent" than divers who used the U.S. Navy diving tables.

Today we recognize that divers who use dive computers are no more likely to get decompression sickness than divers who use dive tables. One big safety advantage of computers is that they make all their calculations automatically and without arithmetic errors. Most dive computers have been subjected to rigorous testing to validate the mathematical models they use.

We don't know for certain how many certified divers there are in the U.S., or how many dives they make, but back in 1986 there were only 351 reported cases of decompression sickness. In 1998, there were 431 reported cases of decompression sickness. Given that our methods of collecting information on diving accidents are much better today, that there are more people diving with a greater awareness and understanding of decompression sickness, there is probably no statistically significant difference between the accident rate then and now. We do know that the number of divers using dive computers in 1987 was only about 15% of the population, while today, more than 60% of the divers rely on a computer for their no-decompression calculations.

Why use a dive computer?

The original U.S. Navy decompression tables were designed for military use, where the typical dive involved sending a working diver to a particular depth to do a job and keeping him there for the entire time. That type of dive profile is known as a "square profile dive," as opposed to the type of diving

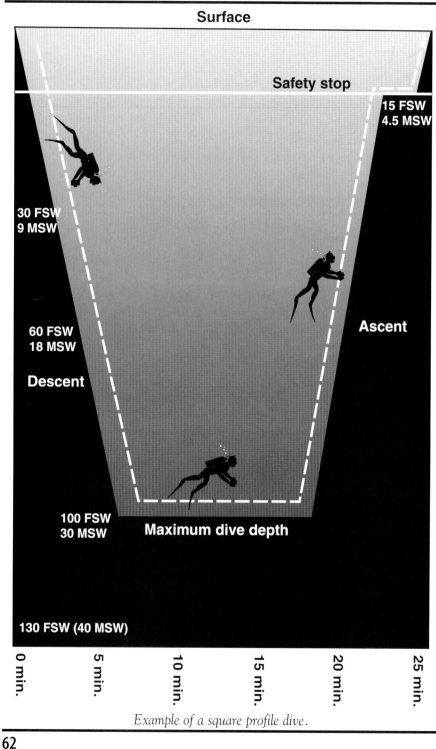

Surface

Safety stop

15 FSW
4.5 MSW

30 FSW
9 MSW

60 FSW
18 MSW

Ascent

Descent

100 FSW
30 MSW

Maximum dive depth

130 FSW (40 MSW)

0 min.

5 min.

10 min.

15 min.

20 min.

25 min.

Example of a square profile dive.

most of us do for fun, which are referred to as "multi-level dives."

On a multi-level dive, you might typically descend to the deepest depth of your dive and then gradually work your way up into shallower water. If you were using the Navy dive tables, you would be forced to compute your entire dive as though it were spent at the deepest depth you visited. Instead, the computer tracks your dive continuously, calculating your nitrogen absorption and elimination at each point of your dive. Typically, most computers are actually more conservative for square profile (single depth) dives, but give you far more bottom time for a multi-level dive made to the same maximum depth.

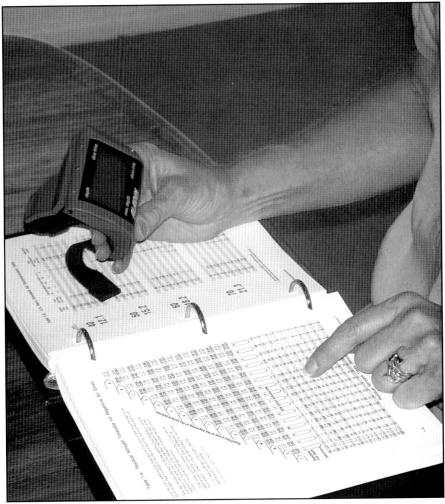

Dive computers relieve you from making tedious calculations with dive tables.

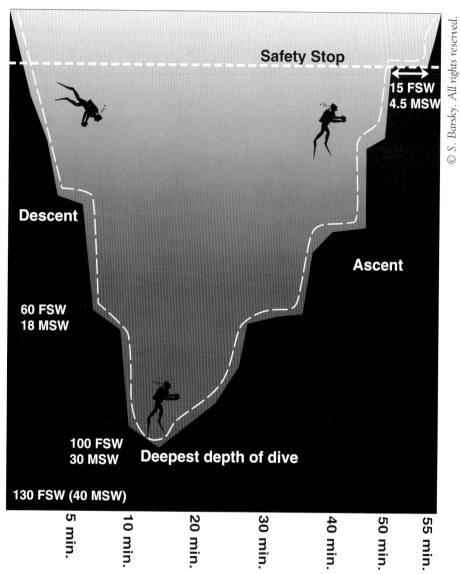

Dive computers allow you to make multi-level dives without unduly penalizing you for the time you may have spent at deeper depths during the course of the dive. They track your position in the water continuously and constantly recalculate your remaining allowable bottom time.

Another advantage of dive computers is that they can calculate your dive profile for "reverse profile" dives without an undue penalty. A reverse profile dive is one where you might start out with a shallow dive first and follow it with a second, deeper dive. If you were using the dive tables in this situation, you would be "penalized" in that your bottom time on your second dive would be severely reduced. Dive computers are generally more liberal in this type of situation.

Although it's always prudent and recommended to adhere to the dive plan you and your partner have agreed to prior to the dive, dive computers give you a way out in the event that you make a mistake or need to modify your plan. The computer makes calculations "on-the-fly" and frees you from the uncertainty of how to proceed if your dive plan must be modified during the dive.

Dive computers free you from having to make tedious mathematical calculations over and over again. Between dives, your dive computer is constantly figuring your maximum allowable bottom time for the next dive, based on your surface interval. By using the planning function in your computer you can run "what if?" calculations – such as, what if you extend your surface interval? – without the need to write down each set of computations.

Today's "air integrated" dive computers sense the pressure in your dive cylinder and compare this to the rate at which you are using the air at depth. These computers will typically display your remaining allowable dive time based on whichever factor is more limiting, either your air consumption rate or your no-decompression status. This type of information can help to greatly increase your safety.

Most dive computers are very simple to use, although they have some extremely powerful functions. If you understand the basics of how a dive computer works, it will be easier for you to make intelligent use of the information it provides and to interpret the data the computer is providing in its display.

"Hoseless" air-integrated dive computers get your tank pressure data from the first stage and receive this information from a small transmitter, like this one, that mounts on your regulator.

Keep in mind that although all dive computers contain similar components and display much of the same information, they all tend to perform a bit differently, so if you buy or rent a different computer from the model you're familiar with, you'll need to spend some time learning how your new computer operates.

What's inside the box?

Every dive computer must have a number of basic components that are common to all models. These include the following:

- **Waterproof case**
The waterproof case is the housing that contains all of the other components of the dive computer.

- **Power Supply**
The power supply is normally some type of lithium battery.

- **Pressure Transducer**
The pressure transducer senses the surrounding water pressure and converts this measurement into voltage that provides an electronic signal that is sent to the analog to digital converter.

- **Analog to Digital Converter**
This device takes the electronic pressure reading and converts it to a digital signal that can be read by the microprocessor.

- **Internal Clock**
This clock measures the time intervals, tells the computer how often to take a pressure reading, keeps track of your surface interval time, and performs other clock functions.

- **Microprocessor**
The microprocessor is the brain of the computer that performs all of the calculations.

- **ROM**
ROM stands for "read-only memory." This chip stores the instructions that are fed to the microprocessor for how to interpret the data it receives from the analog to digital converter and the clock and uses this information to make decompression calculations. The contents of

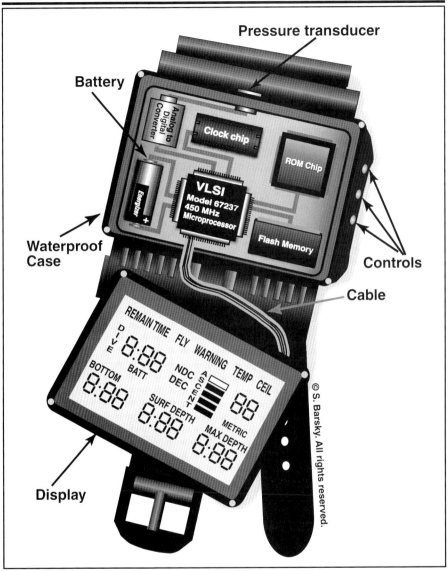

These are the components of a theoretical dive computer.

the ROM chip are "permanent," i.e., when the power to the computer is turned off, the information contained on the ROM chip is not lost. Some models of dive computers can have their ROM upgraded by the manufacturer to add new features as they are developed.

• Flash Memory
Older dive computers relied on "RAM," random access memory to hold

all of the current data from a dive. When the batteries died or the computer was shut down, any information in this "volatile" RAM was lost. Today, most modern computers store a log of a certain number of past dives in a type of chip known as "flash memory." This information can usually be played back on the computer's screen and is not lost when the computer powers down into sleep mode or the batteries are replaced.

• **Display**

The display is where the information from the dive is shown on the screen. You can call up different "screens" that display different types of information.

• **Controls**

Most modern computers have a series of buttons or "contacts" that turn the display on and that you can use to program the computer and/or to "interrogate" it (replay dive data). The contacts can be "bridged" to complete the electrical circuit to activate a particular function by submerging the computer in water, or by touching pairs of contacts with your moistened fingertips.

How does a dive computer work?

Most modern dive computers automatically power up when the computer hits the water, or if it is air integrated, when you turn the valve to your tank on. Some computers today are always "on," keeping track of the day and date, but go into a low power consumption "sleep mode" after diving and the display shuts down until you start to dive again.

Prior to entering the water, it's considered smart to manually activate your computer to ensure that it is functioning properly. When the computer is first turned on, or awakened from sleep mode, it will go through a series of self-diagnostic checks to ensure that all of its components are functioning properly. Typically, all portions of the display will appear on the screen and the computer will count down through a series of tests that usually take less than a minute.

When the computer is first activated on the surface, it will scroll through each ten-foot increment (3 metre) and show you the maximum dive time it allows at that depth. The scroll will go fairly quickly and be repeated on most units. After scrolling several times, most units will go into a standby mode if you don't enter the water within a few minutes.

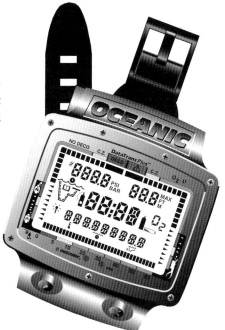

All dive computers run through a self-diagnostic test when they are first switched on. The initial display will look something like this.

When you enter the water, the computer display will automatically turn on, if you haven't already manually activated it, and enters "dive mode" (although some units must be manually activated before you enter the water). Most computers do not begin to record dive time, however, until you submerge below three or four feet (.5-1 metre). This is to prevent the computer from recording any time you spend snorkeling to or from the dive site as part of your bottom time.

When you descend and the computer begins to record depth, it takes a reading usually not less than once every second. The depth reading is sent from the pressure transducer to the analog to digital converter and on to the microprocessor.

At the same time that the microprocessor is receiving the information on your current depth, it is receiving information from the computer's internal clock. It keeps track of your depth and time and compares this information against the information provided by the program in ROM. The computer counts down the remaining allowable no-decompression time for your depth. It will also display the maximum depth of your dive thus far.

As you approach the maximum bottom time for a given depth, most computers will display some type of warning. If you heed the warning and begin to ascend, the computer will recalculate your maximum bottom time for your new depth; taking into account the amount of nitrogen you have already absorbed as well as how much nitrogen you are offgassing at the shallower depth. The computer will automatically recalculate your remaining bottom time through each stage of your return to the surface.

If you exceed the maximum bottom time for your depth, the computer will provide you with a "ceiling," a shallower depth which you must not rise above. This would be your first decompression stop. If the computer displays a ceiling, you should immediately make a normal ascent to this depth and remain there until the computer displays a new ceiling, which will be shallower, or indicates that you are free to surface.

If you ascend above the ceiling before the computer indicates that it is permissible for you to do so, it is quite likely that you will suffer from decompression sickness. This situation is something we refer to as "omitted decompression," which we'll discuss later in this book. Some computers will "lock you out" if you omit decompression and will cease to compute new dives for 24 hours following an omitted decompression incident.

All dive computers track your ascent rate and provide a warning if you exceed the ascent rate specified by the computer's software. Most computers provide variable ascent rates; with slower rates the closer you get to the surface. The ascent rate warning will usually be both visible and audible. If you violate your ascent rate, you must stop your ascent until the computer indicates you are free to resume a normal ascent. Violating your ascent rate increases your risk of decompression sickness.

Once you are back on the surface, the computer tracks your surface interval and calculates your maximum allowable repetitive dive times and depths continuously. The computer will also calculate how long you must stay at sea level before you can fly in a pressurized commercial aircraft with a reasonable degree of safety. If you make another dive, the computer takes into account your previous dive and adds this residual nitrogen time to your new bottom time to calculate the allowable dive times throughout your next dive. If you don't make another dive, the computer continues to calculate the time until it deems that you can fly in a plane, at which time it shuts down or reverts to sleep mode.

What's an algorithm?

When you hear divers discuss dive computers you will frequently hear them refer to the "algorithm" used by a particular computer. An algorithm is nothing more than the particular mathematical formula or "model" used by a dive computer to calculate allowable dive times, required surface intervals, and decompression obligations.

These algorithms are based on theoretical models of what doctors and physiologists think is happening in the human body during and after a dive.

This computer is indicating that the diver has a decompression obligation. The computer refers to this as a "ceiling" which the diver must not rise above. Note the word "ceiling" in the upper right of the display.

Note that the operative word here is "theoretical," because nobody knows for sure the exact mechanism of gas absorption, elimination, and decompression sickness. Also, since everyone's physiology is just a bit different, there is no exact model for **your** particular body. Someday, there may be surgical dive computer implants that provide an exact measurement of what's happening in each diver's body, but for now we must rely on the dive computers that are available.

As was mentioned previously, your body has a variety of different types of tissues that absorb nitrogen at different rates. Tissues that absorb nitrogen quickly are logically referred to as "fast tissues," while tissues that absorb and release nitrogen more slowly are referred to as – you guessed it – "slow tissues."

What's a "half-time"?

Another term that you may hear when divers are discussing dive computers is "half-times." It is not essential for you to understand this concept to use a dive computer, but knowing it will give you a better appreciation for the theory behind dive computer operation.

A tissue half-time is the amount of time that it takes a body tissue to become half-saturated with nitrogen. During each half-time, half of the remaining unsaturated tissue becomes saturated with nitrogen.

A tissue half-time is also the time for a tissue to "off-gas" half of its nitrogen. Each of the different tissues in a dive computer model has a theoretical half-time. These half-times are expressed in minutes.

For example, the U.S. Navy Dive Tables used to use a model with tissue half-times that ranged from a fast tissue with a half-time of five minutes to a slow tissue with a half-time of 120 minutes. It takes a five minute tissue thirty minutes to become **completely** saturated with nitrogen. It takes a 120 minute tissue 12 hours to be completely saturated. Keep in mind that this concept is purely theoretical because there is currently no way to measure a half-time accurately.

Different computers use different decompression "models"

Dive computers from two different manufacturers may use very different mathematical models. Some computers are quite conservative; i.e., they only allow for shorter bottom times and require long surface intervals between dives. Other computers are more "aggressive" or "liberal," i.e., they allow for longer bottom times and only require shorter surface intervals.

Some computers allow you to make adjustments according to whether you feel more liberal or conservative on a particular day. For example, if you didn't sleep as well as you might have liked to the night before a dive, you might want to adjust your computer to be more conservative on a particular day.

When diving physiologists develop dive computer algorithms, one of the decisions they must make is how many different types of tissue compartments they want to take into account in their calculations. Most dive computers in use today are based on a minimum of six different theoretical tissue types, while some use many more. The tissue that is the slowest to "saturate" and "desaturate" with nitrogen will be the limiting factor in your computer's decompression calculations. You may also hear these different tissue types referred to as "compartments," when divers are discussing the theoretical basis for how a computer works.

On deep dives of short duration, the fastest tissues will control your no-decompression time. They will absorb nitrogen quickly at depth and the computer will be indicating that it's time to get out of the water. Conversely, on long duration dives in shallow water, the limiting factor will be the slower tissues.

The differences in the bottom times allowed and the surface intervals required by dive computers are governed largely by the tissue saturation and desaturation times used by the algorithm. Some of the mathematical models consider your body to be completely free of nitrogen after as little as 12 hours on the surface, while others may continue to "carry" residual nitrogen for up

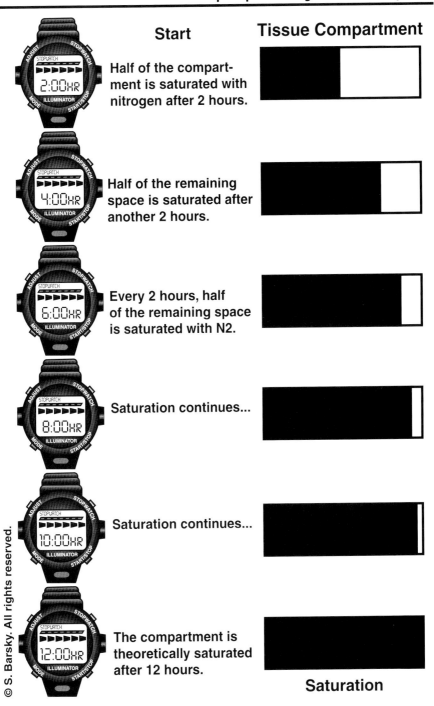

Start	Tissue Compartment

Half of the compartment is saturated with nitrogen after 2 hours.

Half of the remaining space is saturated after another 2 hours.

Every 2 hours, half of the remaining space is saturated with N2.

Saturation continues...

Saturation continues...

The compartment is theoretically saturated after 12 hours.

Saturation

Tissue half-times for a theoretical 12 hour compartment.

to 48 hours following a series of diving days.

Which decompression model is the "best?"

Divers will frequently ask their instructor which is the "best" dive computer. Unfortunately, there is no easy answer to this question. The key to this issue lies in how conservative you want to be when you dive and how much risk you are willing to accept. A more aggressive dive computer might be better suited to a younger diver who is in excellent physical condition, while a more conservative computer may be a good choice for an older diver who is not in the best of shape.

Some of the more common decompression models that are used in dive computers today include the Modified Haldanean Model, the Buhlmann Model, the Reduced Gas Bubble Model, and the DSAT Model.

• The Modified Haldanean Model

Dr. John Scott Haldane was a British physiologist who developed the first set of decompression tables in 1908. Haldane proved that after absorbing an inert gas, like nitrogen, under pressure, the body could stand a pressure reduction of two to one without the formation of bubbles. Some dive computers today continue to use a modified version of Haldane's original calculations, which all subsequent decompression models still have as their base.

• The Buhlmann Model

Dr. Albert A. Buhlmann was a Swiss physiologist who developed a decompression model that has been used in a modified form in many popular dive computers. His work was originally done for high-altitude lake diving. Buhlmann's most advanced work, before his death, was used as the basis for the widely popular Uwatec dive computers.

• The Reduced Gas Bubble Model

Dr. Bruce Wienke in the U.S. developed this model, originally in work done for Scubapro. This model is very sensitive to multi-day and repetitive diving scenarios.

• The DSAT Model

Raymond Rogers and Michael Powell developed an aggressive decompression model that only requires short surface intervals and allows for rapid nitrogen desaturation.

Most dive computers, and their algorithms, have been tested by having divers make dives and recording their bodies' reactions following the dive. One of the most important instruments used to take these measurements is known as a "Doppler flow meter." The Doppler flow meter is used to detect bubbles flowing within a diver's blood stream by the sound they make within the body. The Doppler (as it's usually abbreviated) can even detect silent bubbles (also sometimes referred to as "sub-clinical bends") before the diver suffers from decompression sickness. Doppler flow meters have played a crucial role in helping diving scientists develop dive computers.

What factors should you consider in selecting a dive computer?

Aside from the model that the dive computer uses to calculate your allowable dive times, there are many other factors that you should consider when selecting a dive computer. These factors include the size of the computer, the display, range of information, ease of use, battery type, auto-on/off, controls, programmability, environmental awareness, air integration, lockout restrictions, PC interface, case construction, mounting options, and warranty. It may be impossible to find a computer that has all of the features that you want, and you may need to make some compromises to select the computer that will work best for your particular type of diving.

The ultimate in compact dive computers today actually double as wristwatches.

You should consider all of the computer features described below before making a purchase decision.

Size of the computer

Ideally, you want the smallest, lightest dive computer available that still has a legible display.

Display

The display or screen is the primary interface between you and your dive computer. The numbers must not only be large enough to read, but they must also be presented in a way that makes the information easy to understand. If the information is confusing, you could make a mistake in your diving procedures.

Almost all dive computers have a backlight feature for the display to make it readable under low light conditions. It should be easy to operate the backlight even if you are wearing gloves.

LCD screens are quite vulnerable to damage from sun or impact. The computer should be equipped with some type of protective screen or cover for the LCD that can be removed and replaced if it is scratched or damaged. The computer should not be left where bright sunlight is focused on the display or it could be damaged.

Range of Information

The computer should provide lots of information, but you don't want it all on one screen. For example, during your dive, you need to know your current depth, your maximum depth, your bottom time, and your remaining allowable bottom time. You might also want to know the water temperature, and if the computer is air integrated, you'll certainly want to know your remaining air pressure.

You should be able to access log functions directly from the computer without having to download the data to a PC. The log should provide you with detailed information from your dive, much more than the data that is displayed during the dive itself.

Ease of Use

The computer should come with a good manual that explains its functions simply. However, the computer should be so straightforward to use that you rarely need to refer to the manual.

Modern dive computers have many different functions. You'll want to acquaint yourself with all of them.

Battery Type

The battery should either be a user replaceable, commonly available battery, or an extended life battery in computers that can be returned to the manufacturer for battery replacement. In the event that the battery compartment floods, the computer should not be ruined. Remaining battery life should be displayed only when the computer starts up or the power remaining is low. A computer with a dual battery system that automatically switches to a fresh battery when the first one runs low would be a good choice. Always be sure to check the status of your battery prior to taking a dive trip.

Auto On/Off

Almost all dive computers today turn on automatically when you enter the water. This is a feature that's considered highly recommended.

Controls

Early dive computers had no user programmable settings or detailed log data. Modern computers have many more functions, and to access these features the computer must have control "buttons" or "contacts."

The controls should be easy to activate and labeled. Most dive computers use three "bridge contacts" that must be activated in a variety of different combinations to access different functions.

Programmability

Many dive computers today have user programmable features. Some of the more desirable functions that you might want to be able to adjust or access according to your personal diving style include:

- Altitude adjustment (most computers adjust for this automatically)
- Backlight (the amount of time the backlight remains on)
- Nitrox mix (if the computer is a nitrox capable unit)
- Low air alarms (on air integrated models)
- Conservative or aggressive dive style
- Metric or imperial measurements
- Dive planning and simulation
- Date and time adjustments
- Planning functions
- Depth alarms

Environmentally Aware

Some computers are environmentally "aware," i.e., they sense the surrounding water temperature and make automatic adjustments to the allowable dive time according to the water temperature. Computers that function in this way typically decrease the maximum allowable bottom time in colder waters. Some also automatically know whether the user is diving in salt or fresh water, or whether you are at altitude.

Air Integration

Air integration is an increasingly popular feature found in many dive computers. Manufacturers have developed two different types of air-integrated systems; one type uses a conventional high-pressure hose and the other uses a hose-less transmitter.

Systems that use a conventional high-pressure hose, in most cases, look like a traditional dive console, with a slightly larger than usual computer. Since the computer is mounted on the hose, you don't have to wear it on your wrist, which is a good option if you're the type who makes a habit of reaching into deep holes to grab lobsters.

Hose-less transmitter systems include a special pressure transducer/transmitter that connects to the high-pressure port on the first stage of your regulator. The transmitter sends an electronic signal to the computer that provides the air pressure information. These systems work well, although some suffer from interference from electronic underwater flash systems when used by underwater photographers. The firing of the flash may temporarily interrupt the signal from the transmitter, but normally this disruption lasts for no more than a few seconds.

Some air integrated dive computers will also take into account high air consumption rates and decrease your maximum allowable bottom time because the computer will assume that you are working hard and absorbing more nitrogen.

Lockout Restrictions

Different models of computers have different methods of handling "violations" of the model, depending on what type of "sin" you commit, i.e., whether you exceed the maximum operating depth, or enter a decompression situation, etc. For example, if you accidentally omit required decompression, most computers will completely "lock you out" from diving for the next 24 hours.

PC Interface

Another great feature of many modern dive computers is their ability to interface with a personal computer. To access this capability you must purchase special software and a cable.

Once you download the information from your dive computer you can see your entire dive profile. The amount of information displayed is tremendous, giving you a detailed picture of each dive you have made.

Many dive computers today will interface with a personal computer to allow you to print out and store your dive data.

Case Construction

Any dive computer you select should have as rugged a case as possible. The case should be resistant to shock, vibration, and deterioration caused by ozone.

Mounting Options

Depending on the type of diving you do, you may want to mount your dive computer on your wrist, on your buoyancy compensator using a retractor, or on your high-pressure hose. Check to see what mounting options are available for the computer that interests you. This is a matter of personal preference, but it's nice to have options.

Warranty

Check to see how long the warranty provided by the manufacturer lasts. Also, be sure to see what items and conditions are covered by the warranty.

Scuba I.Q. Review

Dive computer models change regularly. If you already own a computer, take the time to review the manual and be sure you understand it. If you are going to purchase a computer, review the currently available models of computers with your instructor to understand what's available before making a purchase. Take this book with you and use this chapter in evaluating any computer you're considering buying. Be sure you can understand and answer the following questions about any computer you own or are contemplating getting.

1) List three reasons for using a dive computer.

2) List five of the parts of a dive computer.

3) Define the term "ceiling" as it applies to a dive computer.

4) Define the term "algorithm."

5) List two of the models used in modern dive computers.

6) List five factors that you should consider when purchasing a dive computer.

Notes:

Chapter 6
Using Your Dive Computer

Before you ever attempt to use your computer underwater, you must take the time to read the manual. Modern dive computers have so many functions, it is unreasonable to expect to be able to access all of them unless you take the time to read the manual. Have your computer with you as you read the instructions and practice making it perform the tasks you want it to do. If you go on a dive trip, put your dive computer manual in a plastic bag with your dry gear and take it with you so that you can refer to it if you need to between dives.

When you use a dive computer you have to be at least a little smarter than the computer. For example, the computer has no way of knowing if you are dehydrated or failed to get enough sleep the night before a dive. It can't tap into your body to see how you are feeling and adjust itself.

You must be familiar enough with how your computer works to recognize if it is not operating properly or giving you "bad" information. If you always blindly follow your computer, without understanding it, you run the risk of encountering problems in your diving.

Personalizing your dive computer

If your computer has user programmable settings, you'll want to take the time to adjust these before you use the computer for the first time. Do you want the backlight feature to stay on longer, or to set a daily alarm? Make these settings while you have the time to comfortably adjust them.

If you read the manual but you're unclear about how to set your computer up correctly, ask your instructor or the staff of the dive store where you purchased it. Be sure that you understand what changes you are making and that the changes you have made are working correctly.

Basic use of your dive computer

Even though most dive computers have an auto-on function, you should turn the computer on manually prior to entering the water. If you haven't been diving in awhile, be sure to test your computer a few days before your trip to be sure that it's working properly and you have sufficient battery power for the diving you have planned.

If you're going on a dive trip to a remote location, always be sure to take a spare battery along for your computer. Most dive computer batteries are not readily available off-the-shelf items, so you should always carry a spare with you.

Prior to the start of each diving day, if your computer display is not already on, be sure to activate it. Watch the computer as it goes through its self-diagnostics to make sure it is operating properly. Check the status of the battery and make sure that you have sufficient power to make the dives you have planned for the day. Don't try to cut it close and squeeze every last drop of power out of a battery. It's better to replace a battery before it dies than to wait until it fails completely. If the battery fails and you don't have a back-up computer you will be unable to dive until your body is completely free of nitrogen, which for some computers means you'll need to wait 24 hours before you can dive again.

Some older models of dive computers must be manually activated before you submerge for your first dive. If you fail to do this, these models cannot be turned on underwater and you will not have an accurate record of your dive.

Watch your computer scroll through the maximum dive times for each depth. If this is your first dive of the day, and you have no residual nitrogen from prior dives, the scroll will show you the maximum dive time available for each depth. If you have residual nitrogen in your system, you can use the planning function of your computer to see what will happen if you extend your surface interval so that you can make a longer dive.

Compare your computer's scrolling dive times to your dive partner's dive computer if you aren't using identical models. In most cases you'll find that the allowable dive times are quite different. Even if you both are using the same type of computer, manufacturers frequently upgrade the computer or change the software, so your dive times may still not be identical. Plan your maximum dive time according to whichever computer is the most conservative, either yours or your partner's. If your computer is equipped with a maximum depth alarm, it should be set to the depth you and your buddy have agreed upon.

Each diver must be equipped with their own dive computer. It is not safe for two divers to share a single computer, since it is almost impossible for two

Most computers will scroll through the allowable dive times when they first "boot up." You can also check the dive times for each depth at any time while you are on the surface by accessing the planning function.

divers to match their depths perfectly throughout a dive. You also cannot loan your computer to another diver in the middle of a trip so that they can dive while you remain on the surface.

During the dive

Monitor your dive computer during your descent to the bottom. It's important not to overshoot your planned maximum depth. Although most dive computers are equipped with audible alarms, if you are wearing a thick wetsuit hood you may find it difficult (or impossible) to hear the alarm unless you are specifically listening for it.

During the dive, check the computer every few minutes, paying particular attention to your remaining allowable bottom time. It is very important that you do not dive your computer right up to the maximum no-decompression limit for a particular depth. If you have a problem and are unable to leave the bottom when your bottom time is up, you could put yourself in a situation where decompression is required.

Ascending from the dive

Prior to starting your ascent from the bottom you must locate your dive computer in a position where you can observe it continuously as you come

If you ascend too quickly, your computer will display a visual warning and most will sound an audible alarm, too.

up. It's almost impossible to make a proper ascent without monitoring your computer.

Dive computers typically require extremely slow ascent rates and in most cases, these rates slow even more the closer you get to the surface. Some computers will display your ascent rate based on a percentage of the maximum allowable speed, i.e., 90% indicates that you are ascending at 90% of the maximum allowable ascent rate. Other computers provide a graphical display that will indicate whether you are going the correct speed or too fast. If you violate the ascent rate you increase your risk of suffering from decompression sickness.

If you exceed the maximum ascent rate your computer will signal you that you have committed a violation. Most computers will provide a visual warning where the display will flash as well as an audible warning. Keep in mind however that it may be difficult to hear the audible alarm if you are wearing a hood.

In a situation where you have exceeded your maximum allowable depth and/or bottom time, and find yourself in a decompression scenario, the computer will indicate a "ceiling," which is your first decompression stop. You must not rise above the ceiling until the computer indicates that it is permissible for you to do so.

The computer may also notify you when you are below the "floor," the depth below which you should not descend when you are making your decompression stop. If you descend below the floor it is possible you may take on additional nitrogen, rather than relieving excess nitrogen, thus further increasing your decompression obligation. Even though your decompression time will not increase as long as you are above the floor, it will take longer to decompress if you are closer to the floor than you are to the ceiling.

On a normal dive, where you do not have any required decompression, you should still always make a precautionary decompression stop (safety stop) at a depth of 10-15 feet (3-4.5 metres) for 3-5 minutes.

Multi-level diving

The most basic use of a dive computer would be to make a dive to your maximum planned depth, ascend to your safety stop, complete your stop, and exit the water. Although it's perfectly acceptable to use your dive computer in this fashion, you won't be taking advantage of the true power of the dive computer, which is to use it for "multi-level diving."

If you want to maximize your dive time, the best way to do so is to make a multi-level dive where you start your dive at your deepest planned depth and gradually work your way shallower. This type of dive profile works for most open water diving situations. The computer takes into account the fact

If you find yourself in an unplanned decompression situation, the computer will notify you if you are below the "floor," or the maximum depth you must not descend below. In this example, the floor is 10 feet (3 metres), indicated by the upward pointing triangle and the word "ceiling."

that as you work your way up to shallower depths, you are slowly decompressing, allowing excess nitrogen to exit your body at a controlled rate.

As an example, suppose you are planning a dive on a large wreck, a World War II destroyer, that sits upright on the bottom in 140 FSW (43 MSW). The propellers are the deepest part of the wreck and they are 10 feet above the bottom at 130 FSW (40 MSW), while the wheelhouse. where the captain steers the boat, sits at 50 feet (15 MSW). On the deck, between the props and the wheelhouse are several large guns at a depth of 80 FSW (24 MSW).

A good dive plan might be to swim down to photograph the propellers first at 130 (40) and then ascend to the guns at 80 (24), take a few more photos, and then continue on up to the wheelhouse at 50 (15), before making a safety stop at 15 FSW (4.5 MSW). Your total allowable dive time would be much longer than if you spent your entire dive at the propellers, and then ascended directly to your safety stop.

Reverse dive profiles

In the past, diving medical authorities maintained that it was essential for you to always start your dive at the deepest point and work your way shallower. In addition, it was considered crucial that you always make your deepest dive of the day first, and that each successive dive should be made in progressively shallower water. The logic behind this was that by making progressively shallower dives, you would follow a natural profile of decompression. If you violated this type of dive sequence, i.e., started shallow and then went deep, it was thought that you increased your chances of suffering from decompression sickness. This type of diving has been known as a "reverse profile dive."

Based upon the experience of hundred of thousands of divers who have made millions of dives with dive computers, we now realize that is possible to make reverse profile dives, with a reasonable degree of safety, under the following conditions:

- The dives must not exceed the maximum recommended sport diving depth limit of 130 FSW (40 MSW).

- The difference in depth differentials on a single dive, or between dives, must not exceed 40 FSW (12 MSW). For example, if you spend the first half of your dive at 40 feet (12 MSW), you can still descend to 80 FSW (24 MSW on the same dive. Or, if you make a dive where your deepest depth is 60 FSW (18 MSW), you can make your next dive

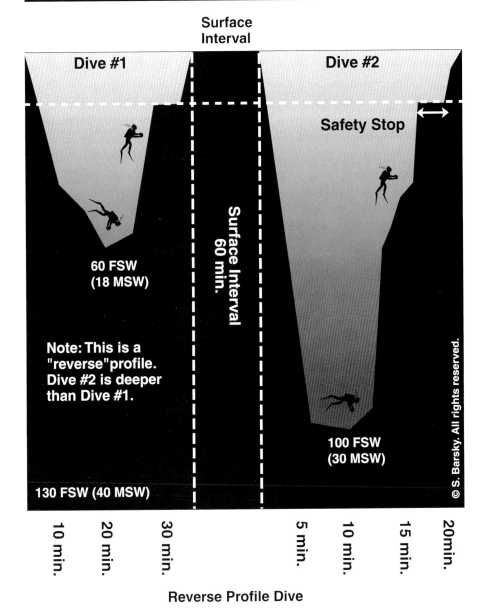

Reverse Profile Dive

deeper, provided your maximum depth does not exceed 100 FSW (30 MSW).

• Of course, your dive computer must indicate that you can make the dive without creating a decompression obligation for yourself.

While it's considered acceptable to make reverse profile dives, keep in mind that in most situations, you will still get the maximum amount of bottom time on an individual dive if you start your dives in deep water and work progressively shallower.

Another type of reverse profile dive that is to be avoided is what is known as a "yo-yo" dive, where you make multiple ascents and descents on the same dive. This type of dive profile greatly increases your chances of suffering from decompression sickness.

Planning Functions

Most current models of dive computers have a planning function that allow you to check to see what happens if you extend your surface interval between dives. We'll discuss this further in the next chapter on dive planning.

Violation Modes

Different models of dive computers have different ways that they handle "violation modes," events that the computer deems unsafe. You must understand when the computer is communicating this information to you, what the information means, and how to deal with it.

Exceeding the Maximum Ascent Rate

All dive computers will warn you when you exceed their maximum ascent rate. Some will require you only to slow down, while others will stop your ascent for varying amounts of time, until the computer calculates it is safe for you to resume your ascent.

Omitted decompression

Many dive computers will "lock you out" from further diving for at least 24 hours if you fail to make required decompression stops. For example, some will only act as a depth gauge and timer, but will not provide decompression information. With most computers there is a "grace period" between the time that the computer senses that you have omitted decompression and the time it locks you out from further diving. This grace period is normally several minutes long, which is theoretically enough time to secure another tank and return to depth to fulfill your decompression obligation.

Exceeding maximum depth

Almost all dive computers will lock you out if you exceed the maximum

Omitted decompression is considered an extremely serious violation and most dive computers will "lock you out" from further use for at least 24 hours after this type of violation occurs. This computer is in violation mode, indicated by the word "Er."

operating depth of the computer. Since this depth is far deeper than the recommended sport diving depth limit of 130 FSW (40 MSW) this is not normally a problem for most divers.

Avoid multiple deep dives with short surface intervals

Just because the computer tells you that you can make a particular dive, it doesn't always mean that it's safe or smart to do so. Making multiple deep dives (below 60 FSW or 18 MSW) with short surface intervals between them is not the best way to dive. This practice may increase your susceptibility to decompression sickness.

Time to fly

Virtually all dive computers available today will provide you with some type of indication as to when the computer has calculated that your body is clear of excess nitrogen and it is considered theoretically acceptable to fly in a pressurized airplane. Of course, the more time you have spent diving and the deeper your dives, the longer it will take for your computer to signal you that you have "off-gassed" sufficient nitrogen to fly.

Depending on the model, some dive computers will allow you to fly in as little as 12 hours or less, while other dive computers require a minimum of 12 hours or longer to fly. If you have been on a multi-day dive trip where you have done lots of diving, it is advisable to wait at least 12 hours to fly after

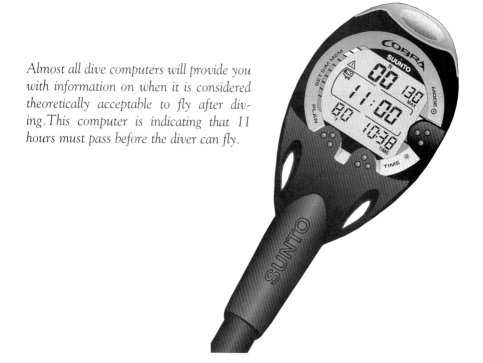

Almost all dive computers will provide you with information on when it is considered theoretically acceptable to fly after diving. This computer is indicating that 11 hours must pass before the diver can fly.

diving. Conservative divers may prefer to wait 24 hours. Again, the computer has no way of measuring whether you have actually off-gassed sufficient nitrogen to fly safely, or if you have silent bubbles in your body that may grow at reduced pressure.

Flying before your dive computer indicates that it is acceptable to fly places you at extreme risk of decompression sickness. As the pressure on your body is reduced as the plane climbs to altitude, it is easier for nitrogen to come out of solution and for bubbles to form in your body. Many divers have suffered from decompression sickness because they have flown too soon after diving.

If you live in an area like southern California, you must also be cautious if you have been diving in the ocean and live at an elevated altitude inland, or must travel over the coastal mountain range to reach your home inland. Even though some of these ranges are only a few thousand feet high, they can cause problems for a diver who has a high load of residual nitrogen in his body from deep diving. Divers returning from Catalina Island have been bent driving in their cars over some of the elevated grades on the outskirts of Los Angeles County.

Diving at altitude

If you plan on using a dive computer at altitude, you must ensure that your computer either automatically adjusts for the reduced pressure at altitude, or that you can properly set it for the altitude where you plan to dive.

Some dive computers sense the altitude continuously, even while they are in sleep mode. With this type of computer, you can dive immediately upon arriving at altitude, although the computer will treat your first dive as a repetitive dive, even if you have not been diving within the past day. This is due to the fact that your body has more nitrogen in it at sea level than at altitude.

Other models of computers do not sense pressure continuously, but must be set for altitude upon your arrival. With this type of system you must wait at least three hours until your body acclimates to the new pressure before making your first dive.

If you plan on regularly diving at both sea level and at altitude, you may want to select a computer that automatically senses altitude at all times. With this type of system it's impossible to make a mistake and forget to adjust your computer for altitude.

If you plan to dive at altitude, you must take a course to learn how to do this type of specialized diving.

Maintaining your dive computer

Although dive computers are built to withstand quite a bit of abuse, they are expensive instruments and should be handled as carefully as possible. Few things are more frustrating than having your computer quit in the middle of a dive trip. Since having your computer function properly is critical to your safety, you'll want to take good care of it.

Be sure to rinse your computer thoroughly at the end of each diving day. If at all possible, soak your computer in clean fresh water for an hour after diving in salt water.

Avoid leaving your computer in the sun for extended periods of time. Sunlight can permanently damage the LCD display on your computer. High temperatures can also damage the electronics and/or the battery used in your computer.

Be sure to pack your computer carefully for transporting to and from the dive site, especially if you are traveling by air to a remote location. It's easy for a dive computer to be damaged by other gear, such as the heavy first stage of a regulator. If possible, take your computer with you in your carry-on bag on the plane, rather than sending it with your checked luggage.

Be sure to rinse your dive computer in clean, fresh water after diving.

Downloading your dive data

If you have the download software and cable for accessing the dive data in your dive computer, you should download the information at your earliest convenience. Most dive computers store a limited number of dives in memory and once the storage section is full, the computer will overwrite the oldest dives in storage. Some dive computers will interface with small portable storage devices that will hold substantially more data than the dive computer itself. These systems help to overcome limited storage problems.

The data from your dive is a valuable record of your diving activity. The software will typically allow you to add the other information from your dive including location, the name of your dive partner, your activity, and other facts.

Consider purchasing a back-up computer

Most dive computers are extremely reliable and rarely fail. However, the possibility always exists that your computer or its battery could unexpectedly stop working. If you are going on an extended dive trip, such as on a liveaboard dive boat where you will be diving daily, you should consider purchasing a second dive computer to act as a back-up in the event your primary computer fails. Wear both the back up and your primary dive computer on every dive so that both computers are operating.

Without a back-up system, you will be unable to dive for at least 12 hours, or until your body is free of nitrogen and you can start using a fresh computer or a set of dive tables. With a back-up dive computer, you can simply switch over to using the back-up, which has been recording your previous dive information, and continue your diving.

Scuba I.Q. Review

Review the following questions about dive computers with your instructor.

1) Explain why it is a good idea to power up your dive computer a few days before any dive trip.

2) List two ways a dive computer may signal that you have committed an ascent rate violation.

3) Describe a possible dive profile for a multi-level dive.

4) Define the term "reverse dive profile."

5) What are two conditions that must be met to perform a reverse profile dive with any degree of safety?

6) Describe two different ways that dive computers deal with altitude adjustments.

7) List two reasons to avoid leaving your dive computer in the sun.

8) Explain why it's a good idea to purchase a back-up dive computer if you regularly take extended dive trips.

9) Describe how most dive computers will react to an omitted decompression situation.

Chapter 7
Planning Deep Dives

Every deep dive should have a purpose, a reason for making the dive other than just to "go deep." Deep diving requires additional training, equipment, and preparation, so this is an activity that should not be taken lightly. Planning for deep diving is not complex, but it does require a bit of thought.

In diving, as in your personal life, planning for future events always takes place in different stages. Some portions of the plan are quite long range, while others are more immediate and take place just prior to the dive itself. For example, if you are planning a dive trip on a local boat, you probably already have a good idea about local conditions and gear requirements. However, if you are planning a diving vacation outside of the country, you will probably need to spend more time researching what gear you will need to take with you.

Long range planning vs. short term planning

Many of the elements in your deep dive plan will be evaluated repeatedly at various stages in your planning as you obtain new information. You'll need to discuss these factors with your dive partner as the preparation for your dive evolves.

Long range dive planning might take place months prior to the dive, especially if you will be traveling out of the country to a distant location. This might include research in dive magazines, on the Internet, or the telephone.

Long range planning is usually a continuous process. For example, let's say that you live on the east coast of the U.S. where there are many opportunities to participate in shipwreck diving. As you become more intrigued by wrecks, part of your long range planning might be to purchase a larger dive cylinder, or even several cylinders, so that you will have options for deep div-

If you're planning a dive trip that will involve air travel to the tropics, you might want to purchase a buoyancy compensator that is more compact and packs easily.

ing. Similarly, if you do lots of traveling, you may find that the BC that works well for deep diving in cold water with your dry suit may be a bit bulky for packing for air travel and tropical diving. If you were taking a dive trip to Costa Rica, you might want another smaller, more compact BC for diving with the hammerhead sharks found there.

Short term planning usually occurs during the week prior to the dive. If you go to the dive shop to have your tank filled for a local dive, you will probably discuss local conditions with the store manager. At this point, you probably already have a good idea who your dive partner might be, or you might have to decide who is the most qualified person to join you for a particular dive. For the same trip, the boat you choose might be the only one available for a particular dive, or there may be boats that are better equipped and more comfortable for diving.

The night before the dive is the time to review your plans for the dive. If you are diving from a small boat, the marine weather should be checked to ensure that conditions are acceptable for boating as well as diving.

On-site planning occurs after you've boarded the boat, en route to the dive site, and once you're anchored over the site itself. Even though you might have been diving from this boat in the past, you may find that the equipment aboard the boat has been rearranged, or that something isn't working, necessitating a last minute change in your plan. It's also possible that while en route to the site, a piece of equipment you brought with you is broken or you arrive at the site and the visibility is unexpectedly poor. Issues like these may require a last minute change in your plans.

Preparing your equipment

If it's only been a few days since your last dive, and you know all of your equipment is working properly, then you only need to inspect it briefly before packing it in your gear bag the night before the dive. However, if it has been some time since your last dive, you'll want to pull your dry suit out of the bag and inspect the zipper, seals, and test the valves, connect your regulator, check your mask and fin straps, and any other equipment you intend to use. This type of detailed inspection should be done several days before the dive so that you have the time to repair any items that may need work.

If you have special equipment that you are carrying with you on the dive, you need to spend some time thinking about how it will be used and any special rigging it may require. For example, if you are using a reel, you need to consider how you will fasten it to your buoyancy compensator, how difficult it will be to release it when you are ready to use it, and any special precautions you need to take to prevent it from snagging or unreeling before you are ready to deploy it.

You will probably find that "retractors" will make it easier to handle and rig many pieces of gear. A retractor is a small, spring-loaded reel that will connect to your equipment and hold it close to your body when you aren't

If you are using any special gear, you may want to think about the best way to rig it. For example, it may be convenient to mount a light on a reel.

using it, unwind when the gear is in use, and wind it back in when you release it. You can use retractors to hold your gauges or computer in position, as well as to connect larger reels, lift bags, and other accessories.

If you use a wrist mounted dive computer and you will be wearing a wet-suit, keep in mind that your suit will compress tremendously and your computer will slide around on your wrist if it is not sufficiently tight. Computers with rubberized straps will tend to stay on your wrist more securely, provided you tighten the strap enough prior to the dive.

If you are using an alternate second stage (octopus rig) with an extra long hose, you may want to fasten the extra hose and the second stage to your tank with a length of surgical tubing that's stretched around the tank. You must ensure that the hose is looped in such a manner that it can easily be pulled free with a quick tug. In addition, you should also be able to reach the unit yourself in the event that another diver grabs your primary regulator in a panic situation. Your instructor will advise you on what techniques are used locally.

Any special equipment preparations should be made well in advance of the dive, so that you have the time to carefully evaluate how it will work. Whenever possible, you should test any new items of equipment and practice using them on shallow dives before you attempt to use them on a deep dive. If you wait until the day of the dive to think about your equipment, you're asking for problems.

Smart divers use a checklist when packing their gear for a dive, especially one that involves extra or unusual equipment. Using a checklist will help ensure you have all the items you need to make the dive.

Do you have enough air?

Any time that you engage in deep diving, it's critical that you make sure that you have enough air to complete the dive comfortably. It's better to have too much air (up to a point) than not enough! Running out of air during a deep dive, or even low on air when you don't expect it, is always a bad situation.

Air consumption can be calculated in a crude way by noting how much time a tank lasts for you at 33 FSW. If you can make a tank last for 60 minutes at the surface, the same size tank will last approximately 30 minutes at the 33 FSW (10 MSW), 20 minutes at 66 feet (20 MSW), about 15 minutes at 99 feet (30 MSW), and roughly 12 minutes at 132 FSW (40 MSW). Remember that if you extrapolate in this way that such inexact calculations will only hold true when all factors are equal, such as water temperature,

Most sport divers stay underwater until they run low on air, then they ascend. Technical divers approach deep diving with more detailed planning based on the amount of air they carry.

exercise rate, and fitness level.

Tanks are filled with air, **not** with time, and air is compressible and subject to leaks and uses other than breathing while we dive. If you frequently add air to your buoyancy compensator, adjust the volume of your dry suit, or fill a lift bag, these actions will all affect how much air you have available to breathe.

If you think about the way most people dive normally, they plan their dives according to the depth they want to go to and based upon the maximum allowable no-decompression time. During the dive, however, it isn't always possible to stay for the maximum allowable bottom time, due to differences in the size of cylinder each individual uses and their "personal air consumption." As we've already discussed, personal air consumption is influenced by a wide range of factors including work rate, water temperatures, psychological stress, and so on.

In reality, what people do is that they dive until they start to run low on air, or their dive computer indicates that they are running out of bottom time, and then they start to come up. This is an acceptable way to dive for you as a sport diver, provided that you monitor your air supply carefully and you do not put yourself in a borderline or actual decompression situation.

On deep sport dives, where you have stayed at a constant depth for the entire dive, you must start your ascent back to the surface with more air in your tank than on a dive in shallow water. There are several reasons for doing this. First, it takes longer to make an ascent from a deeper dive than a shallower one and to still hold enough air in reserve for your safety stop. Secondly, if you have a problem during your ascent, and for some reason you are delayed, you will need this additional air to make it back to the surface comfortably. Depending on your depth and other factors, you might start your ascent with anywhere from 600-1000 p.s.i. (40-70 bar) of air in your tanks.

One technique that works well in sport diving, that we can borrow from technical divers, is to make deep dives by following the "rule of thirds." This procedure states that you use one third of your air for descending to the bottom and completing whatever activity you have planned for the dive (such as taking photos), you use one third of your air for your ascent to the surface, and you hold one third of your air in reserve for use in emergencies only. If you use this formula for managing your air supply you will increase your safety greatly.

Once you cross the line from sport deep diving to technical deep diving, you must know your air consumption precisely so that you can calculate how much time you will get from your cylinder(s). Technical divers use mathematical formulas to calculate how much air they will need to make each dive. It is considered "poor form," as well as extremely hazardous, to run out of air or low on air when you have a decompression obligation.

What's your objective?

To properly plan for a deep dive you need to give some thought to what you want to accomplish during the dive. Are you going to take photographs, or explore or map a wreck? Do you want to look for shells or are you planning to observe fish behavior? Whatever you want to do will dictate many aspects of your plan.

Deciding your objective can be a part of long-range planning or can be more immediate. For example, if you've planned a vacation to shoot underwater photos of the wrecks off Bermuda, you may realize that you need to have your underwater camera serviced prior to the trip. You also know that you'll probably want to take a spare o-ring kit for your camera, and that you'll want to buy batteries and film before you depart the U.S. You might also decide that you want a wide-angle lens to get the best photos of the wrecks. These actions are all part of your long-range dive plan.

Changing environmental conditions can frequently make you change your dive objectives. Even though you planned to shoot photos of the deep

Your objectives during a dive will dictate many aspects of your dive plan. For example, an underwater photographer may want to sit in one place to photograph a particular fish.

wrecks, what would you do if you got out to the dive site and discovered there were dolphins cruising on the surface over the wreck? If you're like most photographers, you would probably change your dive plan to take the opportunity to shoot photos of these fascinating creatures.

It's okay to change your objective as long as you and your partner both agree upon the change before the dive and revise your plan accordingly.

The dive platform

The term "dive platform" refers to the boat that you use for your topside support station. Although many deep dives are conducted from boats, in some circumstances, you may find yourself in a situation where you are diving from shore.

Diving from a boat is usually the easiest, and sometimes the safest way, to conduct a deep dive. The advantage of diving from a boat, provided it is of sufficient size and has sufficient resources on board (oxygen, communications, etc.), is that you can surface directly at the boat without having to make a long surface swim or hike down a beach. Of course, it's usually more expensive to dive from a boat and requires more organization and personnel.

In some situations, deep dives from shore are practical. This dive site in the Red Sea provides deep dives within a short distance from the beach.

Another negative aspect of diving from a boat is that many deep sites are far from shore and access to emergency services may be remote.

In some circumstances, diving from shore may be a good option, or the only option, for making a deep dive. For example, if you are diving in a lake, quarry, or spring, in many situations you will be able to drive directly to the dive site and park your car right next to the spot where you will enter the water. In some locations like the Red Sea, or Scripps Submarine Canyon off La Jolla, California, it's possible to dive in deep water quite close to shore. The advantage to this type of situation is that it is usually easy to secure additional equipment or emergency assistance if you need it.

The type of situation you want to avoid is where you must hike in, or swim, a long distance to the dive site where you will make your deep dive. In these circumstances, if you or your dive partner has a problem, it may be difficult or impossible to summon aid, or for rescuers to get to you, in an emergency. In addition, if a piece of gear malfunctions or you have forgotten something, you may have no choice but to abort the dive.

Positioning the dive boat

The position of the dive boat during a deep dive is more critical than it is during more casual diving in shallow water. You'll want to pay close attention when the divemaster gives his briefing so that you understand where the boat is sitting in relation to the actual dive site.

Ideally, the boat should be directly over the site, or slightly down current from it. In this position, you have only a short surface swim to the anchor or descent line, your bottom time is maximized once you have made your descent, and it's easy to get back to the stern of the boat at the end of your dive.

In California, it's not uncommon for the boat to be anchored with both a bow "hook" (anchor) and a stern hook. This helps to prevent the boat from swinging with the wind while at anchor, especially on large boats that have a high profile. Provided there is no current, this makes it easy to get back to the boat.

In the tropics, many dives are made with the boat connected to a permanent mooring, rather than an anchor, to avoid damage to the reef. If the boat is not anchored at both ends, you should be prepared for the possibility that the boat could swing while you are on the bottom, making it difficult to get

Ideally, the boat should be positioned directly over the dive site.

back to the deco bar at the stern. In most cases, the divemaster and boat crew will brief you on this possibility and make you aware of what procedure they want you to use if this occurs.

Evaluating the location and conditions

When you arrive at a deep diving site, after you have listened to the divemaster's briefing, take some time to evaluate the conditions for yourself. Note any unusual hazards and talk with your buddy about how you would handle these challenges.

Tides can play a huge role in any dive, and can alter conditions quickly. This is particularly true in locations like the Pacific Northwest in the San Juan Islands, or on the east coast of Florida, where the Gulf Stream moves in and out from shore. Strong tides can make it very difficult to dive safely.

If you are diving from a small boat or from the shore, you'll always want to check the tide tables yourself to know what to expect. If there is a big tidal difference between high and low tide, you can usually assume that the tides will be strong. Tides are expressed in feet (or metres) above or below a reference point. On the Atlantic coast, the reference point is "mean low water," or the average of all low water levels. On the Pacific coast, the reference point is the average of the lower of the two low tides each day.

High tides are normally "plus" tides, i.e., and will usually be a few feet (or metres) above the reference point. Low tides can be "minus" tides and may be many feet (metres) below the reference point. Most coastal city newspapers publish the times and heights of the tides on a daily basis on the weather page. In coastal areas, most dive shops and fishing stores distribute free or low cost tide booklets.

Although tide tables are useful predictors, other factors can influence the tides and alter them from their predicted range. These factors include barometric pressure, wind, and run-off from rain on shore.

In the tropics, where the visibility is almost always good, how far you can see underwater is usually not much of a factor in planning a deep dive. In colder waters, where the visibility is more variable, low visibility can be a problem if you have not planned for this contingency. It's not uncommon in locations like California to have good visibility on the surface, but poor visibility at deeper depths. If the visibility is poor, getting back to the anchor line can be a real problem, and it may be essential to have a reel and decompression buoy.

At some locations off California, there are offshore pinnacles that reach almost to the surface from very deep water. At spots like Wyckoff Ledge at San Miguel Island, Farnsworth Bank at Catalina, and Begg Rock off San

Dive operations on a deep pinnacle.

Nicolas, divers normally follow the slope of the pinnacle down to their maximum depth and back up again. These offshore pinnacles are swarming with marine life, and the water is usually exceptionally clear. They are ideal spots for multi-level computer diving. In most cases, the use of a reel and decompression line is not necessary or impractical for no-decompression dives at spots like these.

Another technique that is sometimes used for diving at offshore locations such as California's offshore pinnacles is a system known as "live-boating." A live-boat is a boat that is not anchored, but is under power. Frequently at unprotected dive sites offshore, the wave action may make it difficult for the boat to anchor, the site presents too small a target to readily anchor, or the site may be environmentally fragile. In these situations, the captain will often make the decision to live-boat, moving in on the site, putting the engine in neutral, dropping off the divers, and motoring off the site. When the divers surface at the end of their dive, the captain motors back in, cuts the engines, and the divers swim back to the boat.

Topside Support

On many organized dives, and most live-aboard dive boats, there will usually be a certified divemaster aboard to assist you with your diving. Having a good divemaster on board will make your diving much easier and more enjoyable.

On a deep dive, the divemaster may (depending on the experience level of the divers, the location, and other factors) lead the dive himself or remain on board to act as a support person in the event there is an emergency. The divemaster will normally rig up the deco bar and hang-off bottle, and may have additional gear ready to go. The divemaster will also be available to assist people getting in and out of the water.

If you think you may need to use a decompression buoy, be sure to check with the boat crew and make sure they are familiar with the procedures for this type of operation.

Who's your dive partner?

Selecting a competent (or incompetent) dive partner can have a huge effect on your enjoyment and safety on a deep dive. Obviously, you want an experienced and competent dive partner when you're making a deep dive.

Your dive partner should be just that, i.e., a partner and not a person who is dependent on you for their safety. You don't want to be "crippled" by someone who is not sufficiently knowledgeable or experienced, or worse, whom

The divemaster may personally lead the dive or may remain top-side to act in a support capacity.

you have to rescue. This doesn't mean that you can't assist each other with heavy or awkward equipment, but both of you should be proficient in your diving skills and abilities.

Prior to the dive you should discuss the plan with your partner. This is the time to be open and honest about any concerns that you may have about the conditions, your equipment, the dive operation, or any other factors that you feel might affect your safety. It's also the time to ensure that both of you are prepared, both mentally and physically for the dive. Chances are, if you are uncomfortable about any aspect of the dive, your partner is probably feeling the same discomfort. If you have noticed something about the situation that your partner has failed to pick up on, any reasonable person will be glad that you have brought the matter to their attention. Discuss the matter and see how it can be resolved.

There are many aspects to the dive plan that you need to confirm with your partner. Essential aspects that must be discussed and agreed upon include:

- **What time do you want to make the dive?**
  This may be determined for you by the tide, or the amount of time the boat will spend on site, but frequently you will have options since not

everyone can enter the water at once.

• **Will you do a surface swim to a particular descent point or will you descend on the anchor line?**

• **What activities do you each want to do?**
Make sure your activities are compatible.

• **What is the maximum depth to which you are both willing and ready to dive?**

• **Will it be a multi-level dive or one continuous depth?**

• **What route do you want to follow underwater?**

• **Who will lead the dive?**
You can dive side by side, but only one person can be the leader during any phase of the dive.

• **How will you handle buddy separation?**

• **How will you recognize it if your dive partner has nitrogen narcosis and what will you do about it?**

• **What type of alternate air systems is each of you using?**
How will you share air if you need to do this?

• **At what point will you start your direct ascent to your safety stop?**
What will you use as the limiting factor, remaining air supply or remaining bottom time? If you are making a single depth (square profile) dive, the most limiting factor will be your remaining bottom time. If you are making a multi-level dive the limiting factor will be your air supply. Whichever factor you select, be sure to allow yourself plenty of time, and air, to make your ascent and safety stop.

• **If you are using a decompression buoy, how will you deploy it and under what conditions?**

• **How long a safety stop will you make?**

Both you and your dive partner need to be in agreement about the various aspects of the dive.

Never make a deep dive with a person with whom you have no prior experience underwater. A deep dive is not the place to discover that the person is reckless or incompetent as a buddy.

When your deep dive is the first dive of the day

If your deep dive is your first dive of the day, and you have not made any dives in the previous 24 hours using your computer, your body will be completely clear of nitrogen and your dive computer will display the maximum allowable dive time for each depth. Manually activate the computer and check the scroll, comparing your computer against your partner's.

Planning repetitive dives

One of the most powerful functions of modern dive computers is the planning function. This allows you to see what will happen if you extend your surface interval to allow your body more time to get rid of excess nitrogen.

For example, let's say that you have been on the surface for an hour after making an initial multi-level dive to a maximum depth of 130 FSW (40 MSW). You want to make your next dive to 80 FSW (24 MSW) and be able to spend at least 15 minutes at 80 feet. As your computer scrolls, you find that you cannot make the dive you want to do, that based upon the amount of time you've been on the surface you can only make a 10-minute dive.

To make a longer dive you would need to spend more time on the surface. To figure out how much more time you need to spend topside, you simply enter the planning mode of the computer and add time to your current surface interval and check it against the scroll for your next dive. If you haven't added enough time, you can add more time until the dive time you want is shown. You will then know how much additional time you will need to spend on the surface to make the dive you want to make.

Contingency planning

Occasionally, things go wrong during a deep dive, and you must be prepared to deal with these emergencies. If you wait until something goes wrong to figure out what to do it will be too late to respond in an efficient manner.

On a deep dive, the two emergencies that are unique to this type of operation are required decompression and omitted decompression. Of the two, the most serious would be omitted decompression, but required decompression is not to be taken lightly either.

If you find yourself in a situation where decompression is required, this is the scenario where having a hang-off bottle will be essential. Without this back-up air supply, what should be a simple procedure can turn into a full-blown emergency if you run out of air and are unable to secure additional air in a short enough period of time to meet your decompression obligation.

If you ascend above the ceiling allowed by your dive computer, whether accidentally or intentionally, your computer will go into alarm (violation) mode. On an organized dive with the proper support, the only circumstances that should cause you to completely omit decompression are a serious injury, such as life threatening bleeding, or unconsciousness, where you must exit the water for treatment.

Different computers will respond differently to omitted decompression, but most will give you a short period of time, no more than a few minutes to descend back down to the ceiling shown on your computer. If you fail to return to your decompression stop and resume your decompression time during this short interval, most computers will enter a violation mode where the computer functions like a depth gauge and dive timer, but does not give you decompression information.

Once you have omitted decompression situation you have entered a "no-man's land," where your safety is at great risk. There is no way to predict what your individual physiological reaction may be when this occurs. Some divers

Most dive computers will allow you a grace period before they "lock you out" in an omitted decompression situation.

may have symptoms of decompression sickness before they exit the water, while others may escape unharmed. Specific emergency procedures for omitted decompression will be covered in Chapter 9 on emergencies.

Your contingency planning for a case of omitted decompression should include:

- **Preparations to ensure that emergency oxygen is on board**

- **You have reliable communications**
If you are operating from a boat, a VHF radio is a must. If you are operating from shore, a cellular phone will do. Cellular phones are not recommended for use offshore due to spotty coverage and the inability of the Coast Guard to "fix" the location of a cellular phone.

- **You know the location of the nearest operable recompression chamber**
The key word here is "operable."

- **You have a reliable evacuation plan**
For a marine evacuation, the U.S. Coast Guard will provide emergency transport within U.S. waters.

Scuba I.Q. Review

Dive planning can mean the difference between an enjoyable deep dive and one where nothing seems to go right. Work with your instructor to plan the deep dives for your course by discussing the questions listed below.

1) Give two examples of long-term planning that you might do in preparation for a deep dive.

2) Give two examples of short-term planning that is needed to prepare for a deep dive.

3) Describe the "rule of thirds" and how it is used in deep diving.

4) Explain why it is desirable for a boat to be anchored at both the bow and stern during a deep dive.

5) List two environmental factors that could make it difficult to make a deep dive.

6) List five aspects of the dive that should be discussed with your dive partner prior to making a deep dive.

7) Explain how to use your dive computer to plan a repetitive deep dive.

8) Describe how your dive computer will react to an omitted decompression situation.

Notes:

Chapter 8
Making Deep Dives

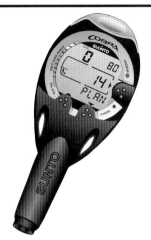

You're poised at the rail of the dive boat, ready to descend to explore a deep shipwreck in the crystal clear waters of the tropics. All of your training and experience have prepared you for this moment and conditions are perfect. You and your dive partner enter the water and descend to the wreck through a vast school of amberjacks, big fish with shining eyes and scissorlike tails. The wreck lies on the bottom beneath you and you can see other divers swimming along its hull. Diving doesn't get any better than this!

Making deep dives is easy when you've got the right equipment, training, and preparation. By the time you finish this course, you'll be prepared to make deep dives under the type of conditions in which you've done you're training.

Keep in mind, however, that if you do your training in a warm water location, it will take some additional training, equipment, and experience to do deep dives in a cold-water location like the Pacific Northwest. It is much easier to make the transition from cold water to warm water diving than it is from warm water to cold water environments.

Gearing up and pre-dive checks

Gearing up for diving should be done slowly and methodically. This isn't always easy to do, especially when you're at a spot where there's competition to get in the water and be the first diver on the site. Underwater photographers are sometimes anxious to get in the water ahead of the crowds, before the bottom is stirred up and visibility is reduced. Other divers have different reasons to hurry into the water.

Frequently it's better to wait a bit and let the anxious divers make their dive than to try to push to the front of the line. Unless you're at a site where there is a short entry "window," you're usually better off to take your time and

Make sure that all your gear is ready to go before donning it.

make sure both you and your partner are relaxed and ready to go at your own pace. You don't want to make a mistake in gearing up for a deep dive.

As you prep your gear, be sure to take the time to review your gear set-up with your partner and note any unusual rigging they may be using. Of course, you should know where all of their releases are located and how to operate them. Naturally, you will test your regulator, power inflator, check your straps, and test your back-up gear before making any dive.

Position the deco bar and hang-off bottle

The deco bar and hang-off bottle will need to be placed in the water. Whenever possible, these items should be hung off the stern of the boat. The lines for these items should be fastened to a "cleat" on the boat. If you don't know the correct way to fasten the lines, ask one of the deckhands to show you the proper procedure for making a line "fast" to a cleat.

Cancelling or aborting a dive

The first most important rule that you must always remember about diving is that if at anytime you feel that something isn't right about a particular dive you can always cancel it, or abort it if it is in progress. You should never feel that there is any shame in terminating a dive. Any experienced diver who has ever cancelled a dive has usually found out afterwards that other people wanted to cancel, too, but everyone else was afraid to speak up. Don't let yourself be forced into a situation where you feel there is no way to back out of making a dive.

Live-boating - at the start of the dive

Live-boating is considered an advanced diving procedure and you must be very alert and in good physical condition to participate in this type of dive. You must pay careful attention to the boat crew who will direct you when it is time to enter the water and when they want you to swim back to the boat when you surface from your dive.

If the dive site does not break the surface, as is the case with some off-shore pinnacles, the crew will normally drop a weighted buoy on the site to mark it. When the boat drops you off on the site it is essential to swim quickly to the pinnacle and make your descent so that the other divers can also get in the water. The boat may be drifting with the wind and if you aren't clear of the boat, the captain cannot reposition it to drop other divers off until you

The hang-off bottle should be in the water before the first diver goes over the side.

have descended. Make your initial descent onto the pinnacle and stop once you get down to 15 or 20 feet. Check to be sure that all of your equipment is functioning properly before continuing your descent.

Making the descent

As soon as you get below the surface, take a moment to check your dive computer and be sure that it is on and recording the dive correctly. If any of your gear is not working properly, the time to find it out is before you race down to the bottom.

Everyone knows that you have limited bottom time whenever you make a deep dive, and the natural tendency in this situation is to descend as quickly as possible. For many divers this is a mistake, as a rapid descent often seems to make narcosis worse upon reaching your maximum depth. Instead, take your descent slow and easy. You don't have to dawdle, but descend at a reasonable pace. Note that the U.S. Navy has used a recommended descent rate of 75 feet per minute (21 metres per minute).

Monitor your dive computer carefully during the descent to ensure that you do not descend below your maximum planned depth. This is especially important if the actual bottom is deeper than you plan to dive. Be sure to adjust your buoyancy as you descend. You want to be slightly negatively

Make a slow descent and monitor your computer closely as you approach your maximum depth.

buoyant during your descent but should be prepared to adjust for neutral buoyancy as you approach the deepest point of your dive.

Be especially cautious as you near the bottom, particularly if you are diving in a lake or other site where there is little water movement at depth. If there is silt present on the bottom you will temporarily limit the visibility if you stir up the sediments lying there.

Wall Diving

Most islands in the Caribbean and far Pacific have coral reefs that surround them. These reefs extend up from the bottom in hundreds or thousands of feet of water, forming sheer vertical "walls." Diving on these walls is an extremely popular form of deep diving due to the clear water, lush marine growth, and opportunities to see large fish.

The procedures for diving on a wall may be a bit different than they are for other types of deep dives, depending on the location and physical geography of the wall itself. Since it's not feasible to anchor a boat on a vertical wall, the anchor is almost always placed closer to shore, with the boat (usually) sitting over the wall itself. In some situations, you may end up diving from a smaller "tender" or inflatable boat, that will follow you on the surface.

Coral walls may rise to within a few feet of the surface or may start deeper. Whatever the case, in most circumstances it's not practical (or even possible) to make your descent and ascent on the anchor line. However, you will have the physical structure of the wall itself to help you maintain an orientation during your dive.

If the boat is anchored over the top of the wall, you can make your descent to your planned depth and then explore in one direction or the other along the face of the wall. If you head off in one direction and the wall is on your right, then the wall will be on your left (or vice versa) as you make your way back to the boat.

The currents along the face of a wall can be quite swift. In most cases, the divemaster will be aware of this possibility and will caution you regarding this when you make your dive. If the current is known to run fast, the boat crew will usually advise you in advance that the tender will pick you up when your surface.

Some people find it especially disconcerting to look out into the blue "void" of the open sea and may even become a bit disoriented. When you are staring out into the open ocean with no frame of reference it's difficult to maintain any perspective on distances, especially when the water is extremely clear. To help regain your orientation, look back at the wall itself and focus on a specific bit of coral.

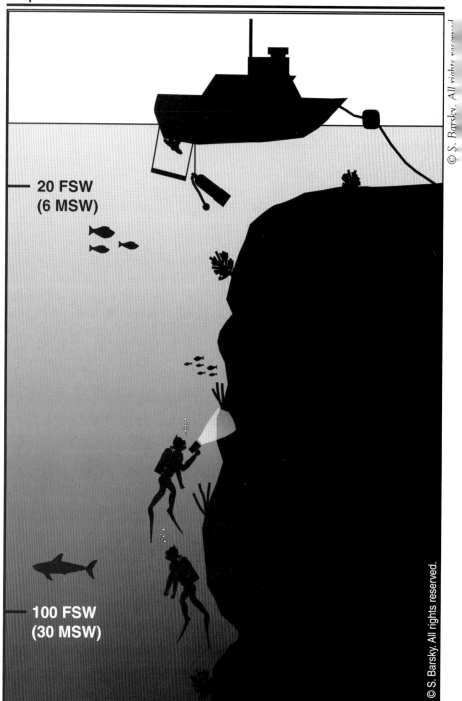

20 FSW
(6 MSW)

100 FSW
(30 MSW)

Wall diving boat operation.

It's not uncommon for divers to have a momentary sensation that they are "falling" when they first descend over the side of a wall. Again, it helps to focus on the wall itself to maintain a point of reference.

Perhaps the most important caution in wall diving is that you must be vigilant about exercising proper buoyancy control and not exceeding your planned depth and bottom time. When there is no accessible bottom below you and the water is exceptionally clear, it is all too easy to dive too deep or stay down too long. Keep a close watch on your computer and be aware of your buoyancy at all times.

On the bottom

Once you reach the bottom, take a moment to make sure you are oriented properly on the site. You want to be sure that you start your dive in the proper direction, depending on the current and other factors.

If you find that you are particularly cold or working hard during the dive, be prepared to start your ascent sooner even if you have plenty of bottom time left in the dive. You do not want to compromise your safety and put yourself in a situation where you are more prone to decompression sickness. If you have an air integrated dive computer that automatically monitors your breathing rate and can detect when you are working hard and adjusts your dive time for this factor or low water temperature, the computer will indicate when it is time to ascend.

Note when you reach the half-way point of your air supply, so that you can allow yourself enough time to return to the starting point, unclip the line (if you're using one), and prepare for your ascent. You want to ensure that you have plenty of air available to make a comfortable ascent.

Using a reel on the bottom

If you are diving on a wreck where the visibility is low, and the wreck is broken up, you should use a line and reel to maintain your orientation to the anchor line. Clip the end of the reel off to part of the wreck, but do **not** fasten the line to the anchor. If your boat drags anchor, you could be injured as the anchor is pulled off the wreck, or you could lose the reel. It's also possible for the line to be cut in this situation.

Pay the line out as your explore during your dive and be sure to keep tension on the line. Do not allow excess slack to feed off the reel. Pay attention to how the line is paid out so that it is easy to retrieve it at the end of your dive and avoid pulling the line over any objects that look sharp that may cut the line.

When you're diving on a wreck, a reel will help you maintain your orientation back to the anchor. This is especially important in low visibility.

Monitoring yourself and your partner for nitrogen narcosis

Whenever you're making a deep dive, it's important to monitor yourself and your dive partner for signs of nitrogen narcosis. If you find that you are unable to concentrate or focus on your tasks during the dive, or your partner appears to be fumbling with his equipment, these are all signs that you should be ascending until you get above 100 FSW(30 MSW).

Adjust your buoyancy

If you are wearing a wetsuit and your dive is to 100 feet (30 meters) or deeper, you will find that the pressure at this depth will compress your suit tremendously. In most cases, you will want to be neutrally buoyant throughout the dive and will need to add air to your buoyancy compensator (or dry suit) to offset the negative buoyancy caused by your weightbelt.

Preparing to ascend

Prior to beginning your ascent, take a moment to locate your buoyancy compensator inflator mechanism so that you have it in your hand. If you are using a dry suit, check your exhaust valve to be sure that it is fully open. You should also have your computer in a position where you can see it continuously during your ascent. Your breathing should be under control and both you and your partner should be ready to start your ascent.

Making your ascent

Ascent techniques vary according to whether you are ascending on a structure, like an offshore pinnacle, using the anchor line, or using your own line feeding off a reel. Each of these methods offers good control both during the ascent and for making a safety stop. Where you dive will dictate which of these techniques are commonly used in your area.

Ascending on a pinnacle or other structure

To ascend from a pinnacle, you simply follow the slope of the structure back to the surface. If the pinnacle actually breaks the surface, or comes close to it, you can usually make your safety stop on the structure. In a situation where the pinnacle does not break the surface, ascend to the top of the pinnacle and then make your safety stop either on or near the buoy. In a live-boat situation there will normally be no deco-bar or hang-off bottle available.

When you ascend in a live-boating situation it is critical that you ascend on the buoy, if present, marking the spot. If you make a direct ascent in open water, it is possible you could surface beneath the boat, which could subject you to serious injuries.

Ascend at the buoy or on the top of the pinnacle, look for the boat once you reach the surface, and inflate your buoyancy compensator just enough to give you positive buoyancy. If the boat crew does not signal to you, it means they do not see you, and you should be prepared to dive below the surface if the boat looks like it is going to run you over.

The captain will maneuver the boat to a position close to you and take the boat out of gear. Do not swim to the boat until the crew gives you the signal to move in. Once you are on the swim step or ladder, quickly clear the entry so that other divers can climb aboard, too.

Using the anchor line to make a controlled ascent

Ascending on the anchor line is a simple matter, except in cases where sea conditions are causing the anchor to heave up and down. In this situation, do not hold the anchor tightly. You could be injured by the anchor line or find yourself ascending rapidly as the line whips about.

Once you have made it up to the depth of your safety stop, in most circumstances you should be able to swim to the deco bar hanging off the back of the boat, to make your safety stop. Be sure to maintain a level depth and do not rise above the depth of your stop.

Using a reel to make a controlled ascent

If you get back to the anchor and find that it is not there, you may need to use your reel to make your ascent. You can use your reel provided there is not a strong current. Your instructor will recommend how to deploy the reel according to local practices.

When there is no strong current, you can make your safety stop on the line attached to the bottom. If the current is strong, you may need to use your decompression buoy to make your safety stop. If you fasten your line off to the wreck, do not attach it to any part of the wreck that might be damaged or break loose.

In a situation where you are making your ascent on your own line, it is essential that you have a true alternate air source for use during your safety stop or for emergency decompression in the event that you have overstayed your bottom time. Without an auxiliary supply you will be placing yourself at risk.

If you are ascending in open water, you must be extremely careful to make a slow ascent.

Ascending in open water

If you have been diving on a wall or in a similar open location where the boat cannot anchor, you must be extremely careful about your ascent rate and making a proper safety stop. This is where mastery of your buoyancy control and careful monitoring of your dive computer become critical.

If you're diving on a wall, you can use the wall in conjunction with your dive computer as a frame of reference and to help gauge your ascent. However, if the top of the wall is at a depth substantially deeper than the deco bar is at the back of the boat, you will have to make an ascent in open water. Be sure to carefully control your buoyancy and monitor your dive computer during your swim from the wall to the deco bar.

At your safety stop

Once you arrive at your safety stop, your objective is to relax, and breathe slowly and deeply. It is important to maintain your chest at the level of the stop, since this is where nitrogen elimination occurs.

If you are clutching a camera or other equipment tightly with one hand, or maintaining a bent arm grip on the deco bar or anchor line, try to vary your hold on these items to avoid impairing the nitrogen elimination from your arm. A tightly bent arm can interfere with normal blood flow, making you more vulnerable to decompression sickness.

When you are hanging on the deco bar or anchor line and there are large swells present, it's better to be slightly negatively buoyant rather than neutrally buoyant, to avoid bouncing up and down in the water. Maintain a loose grip on the bar or line so that you can release it if a particularly large swell moves through.

Avoid swimming safety stops unless the water is exceptionally calm and clear. It's difficult to maintain a constant depth during a swimming stop unless conditions are almost perfect.

If you are nitrox certified and have an enriched air mixture or pure oxygen available for your stop, this is the time to switch over to this other mixture. Nitrox is highly recommended as a breathing mixture during your safety stop.

Keep well hydrated between dives

Be sure to drink plenty of fluids between dives, but be sure to avoid alcohol and caffeinated beverages (coffee, tea, Coca-Cola®, etc.). This is especially important in the tropics where it is easy to get dehydrated.

Dry suit divers in cold climates sometimes avoid drinking liquids to avoid

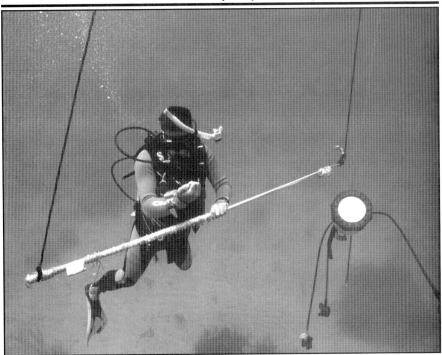

Try to relax as much as possible at your safety stop. Try to avoid keeping your arm tightly bent.

the need to urinate while wearing their dry suits. This is a mistake. Be sure to permit enough of a surface interval to allow time to drink fluids and remove your suit if needed.

Maximizing your bottom time

From a practical standpoint, making multiple deep dives will leave you with very little bottom time and long surface intervals over the course of a day. If your goal is to spend as much time in the water as possible, you'll want to make your deep dives early in the day and follow up with shallower dives as the day progresses.

Scuba I.Q. Review

The mechanics of making a deep dive are quite straightforward. Talk to your instructor about the procedures you will follow for your deep training dives and review the following questions.

1) Describe the circumstances that might lead you to cancel a dive.

2) Describe the procedures for live-boating at the start and end of a dive.

3) List three precautions that must be considered when making a dive on a coral wall.

4) Explain the procedure for using a reel on the bottom during a deep dive.

5) Explain the procedure for using a reel to make a safety stop when there is no current.

6) Explain why making a swimming safety stop is not recommended.

Notes:

Chapter 9
Emergency Procedures
for Deep Diving

While it's rare for an emergency to occur during a well-planned deep dive, it's always possible. Of course, this is one of the reasons why good dive planning is essential. It's wise to discuss possible emergency situations with your dive partner, and to be sure that you both agree on how you will handle the unexpected.

Many dive accidents occur because a number of small problems occur at the same time, or in quick succession, rather than one big catastrophic event. If you continue to dive when you have a small problem, if another problem occurs, you greatly increase the chances that you might have an accident. In sport diving, there is no reason to continue to dive when things start to go wrong. It's better to get out of the water, deal with the problem, and get ready to make another dive.

For sport divers, deep diving emergencies fall into three broad categories; excessive nitrogen narcosis, situations that would lead you to discontinue the dive, and decompression problems.

Excessive narcosis

Some divers are affected by nitrogen narcosis to the point that they are unable to function effectively during a dive. Should narcosis affect either you or your partner in this way, it isn't necessary to abort the dive, but it is important to ascend to a sufficiently shallow depth where you can relieve the effects of this condition.

When you feel fuzzy headed during a deep dive on compressed air and are unable to concentrate on the task at hand, that's a good sign that you are probably being affected by nitrogen narcosis. Similarly, if you observe your dive partner to appear to be gazing off into space with a blank expression, they may also be suffering from the effects of narcosis.

Reasons to abort a dive

There are many reasons why you might abort a dive that is already in progress, although it's unusual when one of them happens. Reasons why you might abort a dive include:

- Rapid depletion of your air supply or loss of main air supply
- Feeling as though the dive has gotten out-of-control
- Exceeding your planned depth or time
- Separation from dive partner
- Loss of reel or parting of line
- Equipment failure
- Unconsciousness

Some of these situations, such as separation from your dive partner, will not require an immediate ascent, but others, such as an unconscious diver, will require you to bypass your safety stop and proceed immediately to the surface.

Rapid depletion of air supply/loss of air supply

You can experience a rapid depletion of your air supply for any one of a number of reasons, including leakage from your gear, heavy work, and/or psychological stress. It doesn't matter what the reason is that you're consuming your air too quickly, but it's critical that you recognize the problem and deal with it promptly.

If you have a major air leak from a power inflator the easiest thing to do is to disconnect the low-pressure hose and manually inflate your BC. A few small bubbles are not a big deal, but a continuous major leak is enough of a reason to terminate a dive.

If you have a leak from an alternate second stage (octopus rig), you won't be able to turn it off unless you are using a double tank system that allows you to isolate the leaking regulator. In any case, these types of situations are serious enough that you should immediately signal your dive partner and start making your ascent.

In a situation where you suddenly lose your primary air supply, either due to a regulator, gauge, or valve failure, if you are equipped with an independent back-up supply, it is an easy matter to switch over to your emergency supply. If you do not have an independent supply, you will need to locate your partner and breathe from their alternate air supply. If you cannot locate your partner, your only choice would then be to make an emergency swimming ascent.

Running out of air on a deep dive is dangerous. If you carry an independent back-up supply be sure it will provide enough air to make an ascent from your maximum planned depth

Making an emergency swimming ascent from a depth of 130 FSW (40 MSW) takes a cool head and skill. If the ascent is executed improperly, you could suffer from a lung over-pressure injury. Even if you make the ascent without hurting yourself immediately, you will undoubtedly exceed the maximum ascent rate required by your dive computer. It's possible you could end up with a case of decompression sickness if the ascent occurs near the end of the dive when you are out of bottom time.

Loss of control

Sometimes you can make a dive where nothing seems to go right, even though nothing major is wrong. While there may not be anything particularly dangerous about the dive, things just don't feel right to you. When this happens it's perfectly acceptable to abort the dive.

Other circumstances may also lead you to terminate a dive abruptly. For example, if you are caught in an extreme current that is carrying you away from the dive site, you should make a normal ascent at the earliest possible moment, so that you can signal the boat to pick you up.

Always remember that as long as you have enough air to breathe, you can work out almost any situation underwater. Slow down and think your way through the problem. As long as you have air, you should be able to make it through the crisis.

Exceeding your planned depth or time

When you reach a point where you have exceeded your maximum planned depth or bottom time, while this isn't truly an emergency, you will probably have placed yourself close to or in a decompression situation. In either of these situations it's time to begin your ascent as soon as possible.

Separation from your dive partner

In shallow water, if you become separated from your dive partner, it's usually not a big deal to surface, link back up, and descend again to complete your dive. On a deep dive, if you become separated, however, it's usually impractical to make a second descent. In most cases, you won't have enough air to make a second descent and you will compromise your bottom time. In addition, multiple ascents and descents from deeper depths are not recommended.

The procedure that you should follow if you become separated during a deep dive, and can't locate your partner in less than a minute, is to surface, link up, and return to the boat. Allow yourself a decent surface interval and plan your next dive.

Loss of reel or parting of line

If you are using a reel and line to return to the anchor line and you lose the reel or the line breaks, you will have to make a decision about how to handle the situation. If you have planned to use the anchor line for your ascent and feel certain that you can find your way back to the anchor without the reel, you may want to attempt to return there. If you have another reel with an "up" line or a decompression buoy, you may be better off in making your ascent from the point at which you lost the reel or the line parted.

This is one of those situations where your decision must be made based on your experience, skills, and confidence. There are no substitutes for these assets in a situation like this. Since each diving environment and dive is subject to a different set of circumstances, this is an individual judgment call.

Equipment failure

While it is extremely rare for diving equipment to fail, it can occur. The most serious problems that could occur in this category during a deep dive would include failure of your BC, dry suit, or dive computer.

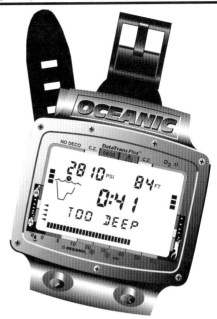

When you have exceeded your maximum planned depth, you will probably find yourself in a borderline decompression situation.

Buoyancy compensators rarely fail in a catastrophic fashion so that they will hold no air whatsoever. In the event you cannot establish positive buoyancy with your BC you usually will still have several options.

If you are wearing a dry suit, you should be using the dry suit for buoyancy control underwater anyway, so establishing positive buoyancy should not be a problem. Put just enough air in your suit when you reach the surface to make yourself positively buoyant for your swim back to the boat. Adding too much air will place too much pressure on your neck and carotid artery and could cause you to black out.

In warmer waters, if you are wearing a wetsuit, your best course of action is to make your ascent on the anchor line, hand-over-hand, if at all possible. You'll want to avoid ditching your weight belt, if your BC fails, since ditching your belt could lead to an out-of-control rapid ascent, leading to possible decompression sickness.

Although it is rare, dry suit zippers and neck seals can fail, which is one of the main reasons to always wear a buoyancy compensator with your dry suit. The buoyancy compensator serves as your back-up buoyancy system. However, even with a complete zipper failure, it is almost always possible to still trap enough air in the suit to make a normal ascent. Should a failure of this type occur, it's time to start heading for the surface.

Unconsciousness

Unconsciousness underwater is a serious emergency and almost always leads to drowning unless the diver is equipped with a full-face mask. It is essential to get any diver who is not breathing underwater to the surface as quickly as possible. There is a risk that the diver will suffer from decompression sickness, and the rescuer will, too, but decompression sickness can usually be treated effectively, while a diver who is not breathing underwater will probably die if not rescued quickly.

Decompression emergencies

There are several types of decompression emergencies that are of particular concern in deep diving, including dive computer failure, unplanned and required decompression, omitted decompression, and decompression sickness.

Dive computer failure

Today's dive computers are extremely reliable, but it is always possible for your computer to stop functioning. Almost all dive computer failures can be traced to either poor maintenance or abuse of the computer itself. Maintenance problems can lead to floods or battery failure. Abuse of the computer includes dropping the unit onto a hard deck or allowing the computer to be exposed to high heat, such as in the trunk of a car.

If your computer fails during a normal no-decompression dive, this is a simple situation. If you're equipped with a back-up computer, you can simply continue your dive. Otherwise, signal to your dive partner and make a normal ascent to your safety stop. Complete your safety stop and exit the water.

When your dive computer fails in the middle of a multi-day dive trip, if you do not have a back-up system you have two choices. If you can rent or borrow another computer, you can resume diving on your next dive to depths not exceeding 20 FSW (6 MSW) for the balance of your trip. Your other option would be to discontinue diving for 24 hours and then start diving with the new computer for the remainder of your vacation.

Should your computer fail during a dive where you find that you have an unexpected decompression commitment, and you do not have a back-up dive computer, you have a more serious problem. If you have maintained good buddy contact, then your dive partner should have the same decompression requirement as you, provided that you both have the same type of dive computer. Communicate your problem to your dive partner and make a normal ascent to your ceiling, timing your stay using your partner's computer.

The worst-case scenario would be to have an unexpected decompression requirement, followed by a computer failure, and find yourself separated from your dive partner. If your dive was originally planned as a no-decompression dive and you have unexpected decompression due to an error on your part, your ceiling will probably be no deeper than the deco bar and your decompression time should be brief. Provided the above is true, make a normal ascent and proceed directly to the deco bar or use your decompression buoy as appropriate.

Remain at the deco bar for the amount of time indicated by your dive computer before it quit, counting off the time to yourself in your head. If you know that your remaining air supply will supply you with more than enough air to meet your decompression requirement, you can simply remain at the deco bar until you have just over 200 p.s.i. (15 bar) remaining in your tank, and surface with sufficient air to inflate your BC or use your air powered signaling device. Keep in mind that analog submersible pressure gauges tend to be less accurate at lower tank pressures.

Required Decompression

Should you accidentally exceed the maximum time allowed by your dive computer for the maximum depth of your dive, you will be in a situation where decompression becomes mandatory. Once you enter a decompression situation, this may be indicated by nothing more than the word "Ceiling" or "Decostop," on the computer display. As soon as you discover this to be the case, you and your partner should begin a normal ascent, watching the display of your computer carefully.

If you accidentally enter a decompression situation, you need to begin your ascent as soon as possible. This computer is indicating that the diver has a decompression obligation at a depth of 10 feet.

Once you reach your decompression stop, maintain a constant depth with your chest at the level of the ceiling indicated by your dive computer. Breathe deeply and relax for the entire length of your stop. Ascend slowly from your stop to the surface.

Omitted Decompression

Omitted decompression is one of the most serious emergencies in diving, whether you have committed this violation of safe diving practices intentionally or accidentally. In an omitted decompression situation it is highly likely that you will end up suffering from decompression sickness.

If you have managed to ignore the alarms on your computer, only to discover once you are back on the boat that you have omitted decompression, you may be able to grab a fresh tank to complete your decompression obligation before the computer locks you out. Notify the divemaster of your problem before you enter the water so that he can enter the water to accompany you (or arrange for someone to accompany you) at your stop.

In a situation where you don't realize your mistake until you have been on the surface beyond your dive computer's grace period, your computer will lock you out. If you still do not have signs or symptoms of decompression sickness you should immediately notify the divemaster. The divemaster will usually instruct you to follow one of two procedures.

Notify the divemaster immediately if you have omitted decompression.

If you are in a omitted decompression situation for longer than five minutes on the surface, you need to be sure to get on oxygen immediately.

• If you have been on the surface longer than the grace period allowed by your computer, but for less than five minutes, you should return to the depth of your missed decompression stop (ceiling) with your dive partner and remain there for 1 1/2 times the required stop time. Obviously, you must have enough air with you to complete this stop. Once you complete this stop, you must refrain from diving until your dive computer clears and indicates it is possible for you to dive again. Some computer manufacturers recommend that you stay out of the water for up to 48 hours following an omitted decompression incident even if you have no symptoms.

• If you cannot return to your stop depth within five minutes of surfacing, both you and your dive partner should breathe 100% oxygen for a minimum of 60 minutes. If you are without symptoms after 60 minutes on oxygen, you must stay out of the water until your dive computer clears and indicates that it is possible for you to dive again. Some computer manufacturers recommend that you stay out of the water for up to 48 hours following an omitted decompression incident even if you have no symptoms.

It's possible that you could begin to suffer from decompression sickness during your ascent, after you hit the deck, or after you have resubmerged.

u start to exhibit the signs and symptoms of decompression sickness you ~~ forget dealing with your omitted decompression problem and start dealing with your decompression sickness problem.

First Aid for Decompression Sickness

The single most important first aid measure for a diver who is suffering from decompression sickness is to get the victim on pure oxygen as soon as possible. By breathing 100% pure oxygen, the nitrogen is drawn out of the body.

With pure oxygen in the lung sacs (alveoli), the nitrogen in the body flows from the blood stream, where it as at a higher pressure, into the alveoli where it is at a lower pressure in an attempt to establish equilibrium. By removing the excess nitrogen, we can slow or halt the growth of nitrogen bubbles in the body. Another benefit of breathing pure oxygen is that in the event that nitrogen bubbles are blocking circulation to tissues, the pure oxygen will (hopefully) diffuse through the surrounding tissues to provide oxygen to tissues that would otherwise not receive normal circulation.

A diver who is suffering from decompression sickness, without serious symptoms, should be instructed to lie on his back while breathing oxygen. The diver who is experiencing serious symptoms (such as paralysis, numbness, etc.) should be instructed to lay on his side, with his head supported and his upper leg bent at the knee. If the diver vomits, this position will help to keep the airway clear.

For divers who are suffering from decompression sickness but are alert and aware of their surroundings, fresh water taken by mouth is also recommended. Water is less likely to lead to vomiting than other fluids and is rapidly absorbed by the body.

Any diver who is suffering from decompression sickness should receive oxygen continuously while they are en route to the chamber. Be sure to send their dive computer to the chamber with them so that the chamber personnel can review the person's recent diving history to assist them in making their treatment decisions.

Every diver should enroll in an SDI CPROX course, that trains you to cope with diving emergencies through the administration of oxygen and cardio-pulmonary resuscitation (CPR). If you intend to become a divemaster or instructor, this training is mandatory.

Recompression is essential for decompression sickness

Once you have determined that a diver is suffering from decompression sickness, it is vital to get the diver to the nearest hyperbaric treatment cen-

The captain is the person who will arrange for evacuation of injured divers aboard a dive boat.

ter as quickly as possible. If you are diving in a remote location, such as from a liveaboard dive boat, helicopter evacuation and air ambulance transportation to the closest chamber may be necessary.

Recompression in the water is neither practical nor safe for divers without sufficient training or resources to accomplish this procedure. Treatment takes way too much time (usually at least six hours) and there is a risk that you could suffer from neurological symptoms that could cause you to lose muscular control leading to drowning underwater. The treatment also involves the use of pure oxygen at depths that would be unsafe for breathing this gas underwater. In cold water, most treatment schedules would also place the diver in hypothermic condition before the treatment could be completed. Even in warm water, body heat loss becomes a problem for a diver during long exposures with no physical activity.

Chamber treatment involves recompressing the diver to a depth sufficient to recompress the bubbles and allow them to properly come out of solution. This is a slow process that usually takes at least six hours, but may be longer and involve additional treatments over several days. Recompression therapy is very expensive and is not covered by all insurance policies. If you plan to regularly participate in diving you should purchase diving accident insurance. Ask your instructor about the insurance plan available through

Recompression treatment is essential for any diver who is suffering from decompression sickness. This is best accomplished in a hyperbaric chamber.

the dive shop where you are receiving your training.

If you do suffer from decompression sickness, a physician who is knowledgeable in diving medicine must clear you for diving before you can participate in the sport again. Most physicians will recommend that you refrain from diving for several weeks after treatment for decompression sickness.

Scuba I.Q. Review

Do you understand the proper emergency procedures for deep diving problems? Discuss the questions listed here with your instructor.

1) List four reasons that might lead you to abort a deep dive.

2) Explain the procedure to be followed if your dive computer fails during a deep dive when you do not have a decompression obligation.

3) Describe the procedure to be followed for omitted decompression when you discover that you have committed this computer violation within the grace period allowed by your dive computer.

4) Describe the procedure to be followed for omitted decompression once

your dive computer has locked you out from decompression calculations.

5) Describe the recommended first aid for decompression sickness.

6) Explain the treatment a diver who is suffering from decompression sickness should receive.

7) Explain why treatment of recompression sickness in the water is impractical.

Chapter 10
Extending Your
Deep Diving Capabilities

Once you learn how to properly participate in deep diving, you'll definitely want to continue to extend your diving capabilities. You will discover that diving is an adventure that has so many different facets that no one person can know everything about it. Check out these additional training courses to learn how you can become more proficient and participate in many different types of diving activities.

Nitrox diving

Nitrox is a gas mixture that divers use in place of ordinary compressed air, to extend their bottom time at depths down to 130 FSW (40 MSW). It is a mixture of nitrogen and oxygen that contains more than the 21% of oxygen found in normal air. The most popular nitrox mixtures for sport diving contain 32%, 36%, 40%, 50%, or 60% oxygen.

Nitrox extends your bottom time because your body absorbs less nitrogen at depth since you are breathing fewer nitrogen molecules each time you take a breath. While dive times with different dive computers will vary, at a depth of 60 feet (18 meters) a "typical" dive computer might only allow you to stay underwater on your first dive for no more than 53 minutes breathing compressed air. However, if you were breathing a nitrox mixture containing 36% oxygen a nitrox computer might allow you to stay underwater up to 90 minutes without the need for decompression stops! Mixtures containing greater percentages of oxygen allow you to stay underwater even longer.

Nitrox is as easy to use as compressed air, but you must understand how to use it properly. There are depth limitations on nitrox according to how much oxygen is in the mixture you are using.

SDI's Easy Nitrox course teaches you to use nitrox without the need to learn complex mathematical formulas. If you can use a dive computer, you

Using nitrox is a great way to extend your bottom time.

can participate in Easy Nitrox Diving. Nitrox is a great way to maximize your bottom time on every diving trip.

Semi-Closed Circuit Rebreather

Ordinary open circuit scuba equipment is extremely wasteful of your breathing gas, whether you are using nitrox or compressed air. Each breath you take is exhaled into the water and escapes back to the atmosphere. Since you consume little of the oxygen that you inhale with each breath, it is far more efficient if you can reuse your exhaled gas rather than "wasting" it.

A semi-closed circuit rebreather is a type of self-contained diving apparatus that uses nitrox as the breathing medium and recirculates each breath you take by passing it through a chemical "scrubber" to remove the carbon dioxide you exhale. Any oxygen that is used is replenished by a slow, but steady trickle of oxygen into the breathing "loop" from a regulator that helps ensure that the correct oxygen level is maintained.

Rebreathers are popular with divers because they are quieter than open circuit gear, allow extended bottom times, and in some situations, permit you to get closer to marine life. Rebreathers are also ideal if you are making an extended trip aboard a small boat, since they reduce the amount of breathing gas that you must carry aboard the boat. If you are nitrox certified, using a rebreather is the next logical step in expanding your abilities as a diver.

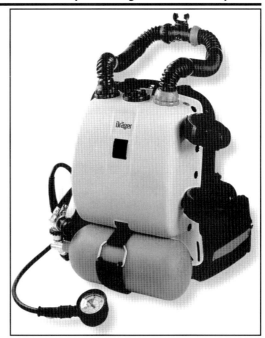

Semi-closed circuit rebreathers offer advantages for small boat diving and underwater photography.

Wreck Diving

One of diving's most exciting activities is exploring shipwrecks, whether you are swimming over the remains of a sailing ship in the Great Lakes or exploring the hulk of a freighter off the Florida keys. Wreck diving is a window into the past.

In the SDI wreck diving course, you'll learn how to properly equip yourself for wreck diving and the techniques that are used to make your wreck exploration more comfortable and efficient. This introduction to wreck diving will prepare you for exploring the exterior of shipwrecks, but is not designed to train you in the more specialized techniques for exploring the interior of wrecks.

Technical Diving Courses

Once you have learned how to participate in deep air dives down to 130 FSW (40 MSW), you may want to extend your capabilities to deeper depths. Technical Diving International (TDI), SDI's sister company, offers courses in decompression procedures, extended range (down to 180 FSW or 55 MSW) and trimix (mixed gas) diving. These courses are beyond the scope of sport diving.

Technical diving is not for everyone. It requires much more discipline than sport diving.

Decompression Procedures

Properly setting up and performing a decompression dive takes planning and discipline. Technical Diving International can provide you with the training that you need to participate in dives that require staged decompression.

In this course you will plan and make decompression dives down to 150 FSW (45 MSW) and learn the proper procedures for using both nitrox and pure oxygen for decompression.

Extended Range Diving

The TDI Extended Range Diving course will prepare you to dive with air down to depths of 180 FSW (55 MSW). In this depth range, all of your dives will be decompression dives and you will utilize the skills you learned in the decompression diving course.

This course is considered a must for any diver who wants to participate in deep wreck diving or deep cave diving. To see the deep wrecks in Chuuk or explore the deep caves of Florida you need this course to further your training.

Trimix Diving

Trimix is a gas mixture that contains three different gases; helium, oxygen, and nitrogen. It is considered the ultimate gas mixture for breathing for deep dives. The big advantage to using trimix is that it virtually eliminates the problems one experiences with nitrogen narcosis at depths below 100 FSW.

In the TDI trimix course you will learn to use this advanced gas mixture to make dives down to 300 FSW (90 MSW).

Scuba I.Q. Review

There are many diving specialty areas that can take you beyond the skills you have learned for deep diving in the sport diving range. Discuss your interests with your instructor and review the following questions.

1) Define the term "nitrox," and explain why using this gas mixture permits divers to stay underwater for longer dives without decompression.

2) List two advantages to using a semi-closed circuit rebreather.

3) List two gases other than air that can be used during decompression dives.

4) List the three gases that are used to make "trimix?"

Notes

For Additional Reading

Bennett, P. and Elliott, D. *The Physiology and Medicine of Diving, 4th Edition.* W.B. Saunders Company, Ltd. Philadelphia, PA. 1993. 613 pages

Bove, A. *Diving Medicine, Third Edition.* W.B. Saunders Company, Philadelphia, PA. 1997. 418 pages

Gilliam, B., Von Maier, R., and Crea, J. *Deep Diving: An Advanced Guide to Physiology, Procedures, and Systems. Revised Edition.* Watersport Publishing, San Diego, CA. 1995, 351 pages

Huggins, K. *The Dynamics of Decompression Workbook.* University of Michigan, Ann Arbor Michigan. 1992

Lang, M. and Lehner, C. (eds.) *Proceedings of the Reverse Dive Profiles Workshop.October 29-30.* Smithsonian Institution, Washington, D.C. 295 pages. 2000

Glossary

AGE
Abbreviation for arterial gas embolism. This is a blockage of an artery by a bubble of gas that was released by a lung over-pressure accident.

air integrated dive computer
A dive computer that includes an additional pressure transducer to record data for air cylinder pressure in addition to decompression information. May also provide information on remaining bottom time based on air consumption, and may consider air consumption in decompression calculations.

algorithm
The mathematical formula or "model" used by a dive computer to calculate allowable dive times, required surface intervals, and decompression obligations.

alveoli
The smallest air sacs in the lungs. This is where gas exchange takes place. Nitrogen is absorbed and eliminated from the body here.

bail-out bottle
A small scuba cylinder, typically 13-19 cubic feet (2-3 litres) in volume, that is used as an emergency supply for deep diving or other diving activities. Bail-out bottles are fitted with their own regulators and the system is attached to the diver's main supply. Also known as a "pony bottle."

balanced regulator
A regulator that breathes as easily at high cylinder pressures as well as low cylinder pressures.

buddy dependent alternate air source
Any emergency air supply that is supplied by your diving partner. In most cases, a buddy dependent alternate air source would refer to an octopus rig or similar arrangement.

buddy independent alternate air source
Any emergency air supply that is carried by the individual diver. Usually refers to a bail-out bottle or Spare-Air® system.

Buhlmann Model

Dr. A.A. Buhlmann was a Swiss physiologist who developed a decompression model (algorithm) that has been used in a modified form in many popular dive computers. His work was originally done for high altitude lake diving.

carbon dioxide

The waste gas produced by the human body by all metabolic processes. Abbreviated CO_2.

ceiling

The minimum depth one can ascend to on a dive where decompression stops are required.

deco bar

A bar hung horizontally under the back of a dive boat to provide a convenient place for divers to maintain a constant depth while completing a safety stop. The bar can be made of any material, although most are made of either plastic pipe or metal. See also decompression bar.

decompression bar

A bar hung horizontally under the back of a dive boat to provide a convenient place for divers to maintain a stable depth while completing a safety stop. The bar can be made of any material, although most are made of either plastic pipe or metal. See also deco bar.

decompression buoy

An inflatable buoy with a line attached to it, that is dispatched by a diver while underwater to provide a stable location to complete a safety stop. A diver would use a decompression buoy to make an ascent where there is no boat to mount a decompression bar on.

DCI

Abbreviation for decompression illness. Term used to refer to both decompression sickness and the lung over-pressure accident that is known as an "arterial gas embolism" or "AGE."

DCS

Abbreviation for decompression sickness. A condition where a diver has excess nitrogen in his blood stream that has formed bubbles that are affecting circulation, breathing, muscle, or nerve tissue.

Glossary

decompression
Every time a diver returns to the surface from a dive he is experiencing decompression, i.e., relieving the pressure that is pressing down on his body.

decompression dive
A dive where the diver has absorbed excess nitrogen to the point that stops must be made in the water to allow this nitrogen to escape the body without forming bubbles.

decompression sickness
A condition where a diver has excess nitrogen in his blood stream that has formed bubbles that are affecting circulation, breathing, muscle, or nerve tissue.

decompression stop
A stop made in the water by an ascending diver for a specific period of time to allow excess nitrogen to come out of solution without the formation of bubbles in the body. These stops are specified either by a set of decompression tables or a dive computer.

deco stop
Abbreviated or slang expression for decompression sickness.

deep-sea diver
A diver who works professionally to conduct heavy work in the ocean. This type of diver wears a special helmet to supply breathing gas and communications.

diuresis
A physical condition where the body circulates more blood than normal through the kidneys leading to a higher than normal production of urine. Diuresis can be caused by cold or consuming alcohol or caffeine.

dive profile
The movement of a diver up and down through the water column during the course of a dive. When plotted on a graph this is a physical representation of the diver's movements in the water.

Doppler flow meter

A device that is used to monitor the flow of blood through a person's body that can also detect the movement of nitrogen bubbles in the blood stream.

driving pressure

Increased pressure of nitrogen (or other inert gas) that causes more of that gas to move through body tissues. During the descent phase of a dive, the driving pressure forces more nitrogen to pass from the lungs into the blood stream. During the ascent phase, the driving pressure forces more gas to pass from the blood stream back into the lungs.

DSAT Model

A decompression model (algorithm) developed for Diving Science and Technology, a business organization in the diving industry.

floor

The deepest depth that a diver can safely descend to without absorbing more nitrogen when that diver's dive computer indicates that he has a "ceiling" (decompression stop) that he cannot ascend above.

FSW

Abbreviation for feet of sea water.

Haldanean Model

Dr. John Scott Haldane was a British physiologist who developed the first set of decompression tables in 1908. Haldane proved that after absorbing an inert gas, like nitrogen, under pressure, the body could stand a pressure reduction of two to one without the formation of bubbles.

half-time

The amount of time that it takes a body tissue to become half-saturated with nitrogen. It takes the same amount of time for the tissue to desaturate.

hang-off bottle

A bottle that is hung over the side of the boat to provide additional air for a diver who is ascending from a deep dive and may need additional air to complete a safety stop or decompression stop. Also known as a "deco bottle."

Glossary

heli-ox
A gas mixture used for deep diving that contains helium and oxygen.

hypothermia
A condition where the body's internal temperature is lower than normal. Hypothermia can lead to problems with thought and muscular control. In extreme cases it can be fatal.

inert gas narcosis
A condition caused by breathing a gas mixture containing an inert gas under pressure. At depth, inert gas narcosis can cause the diver to be confused and have difficulty performing simple tasks by affecting the mind as well as coordination.

life-support equipment
Any equipment that is essential to sustain life in a hostile environment, such as outer space or under water. Breathing apparatus and thermal protection suits are considered to be life-support apparatus.

live-boat
A boat that provides support for diving operations but is not anchored to the bottom. The boat is free to maneuver to pick up divers on the surface.

multi-level dive
A dive where the diver varies his depth at different times during the course of the dive.

nitrogen narcosis
The intoxicating effect of nitrogen at depths approaching 100 FSW (30 MSW) and deeper. Symptoms of nitrogen narcosis can include dizziness, lack of coordination, inability to think clearly, and other symptoms that resemble alcoholic intoxication.

nitrox
Any gas mixture that contains nitrogen and oxygen but has more than the normal 21% of oxygen found in ordinary air.

neurologic decompression sickness
Decompression sickness that affects the nervous system of the human body. Sometimes referred to as "the staggers."

off-gas
The process of eliminating excess nitrogen from the body.

omitted decompression
A situation that occurs when a diver has a decompression obligation but fails to make the appropriate decompression stops.

patent foramen ovale
An abnormal opening between the two sides of the human heart. Suspected of being a contributing factor to decompression sickness in some divers.

pelagic
Used to describe any creature that lives in the open ocean, usually far from land.

perfusion
Circulation of blood to a portion of the body.

PFO
Abbreviation for patent foramen ovale.

pony bottle
Another term used to describe a bail-out bottle.

pulmonary decompression sickness
Decompression sickness that affects the lungs and breathing. Sometimes referred to as "the chokes."

Reduced Gas Bubble Model
Decompression model (algorithm) developed by Dr. Bruce Wienke. The model is sensitive to repetitive dives and multi-day diving.

repetitive dive
Any dive that falls within the period of time where the dive computer or tables you are using considers that you still have residual nitrogen in your body from a prior dive.

reverse profile
A repetitive dive that is deeper than the dive preceding it. This type of dive profile was formerly thought to increase the likelihood of decompression

sickness, but current thinking is that this does not present a problem.

rule-of-thirds
Breathing gas management strategy used for cave diving and penetration wreck diving. One third of the diver's gas is used for descent and time spent at depth, one third of the gas is reserved for the ascent, and one third of the gas is held in reserve for emergencies.

silent bends
Nitrogen bubbles inside the body that do not produce symptoms of decompression sickness. It is generally believed that silent bubbles are present after all dives.

silent bubbles
Another term for silent bends.

skip-breathing
A practice used by some divers to stretch their air supply by holding each breath for longer than normal, prior to exhaling. Considered dangerous due to the fact that abnormal amounts of carbon dioxide are accumulated in the body which can lead to difficulty in responding at high exercise rates during an emergency. Carbon dioxide is also thought to contribute to nitrogen narcosis.

square profile dive
A dive where the diver remains at one continuous depth for his entire time on the bottom.

sub-clinical decompression sickness
A condition where micro-bubbles exist in a diver's body, but there are no overt symptoms of decompression sickness, although the diver may be fatigued. Extreme fatigue, beyond what might be expected from the dive in question, would indicate probable decompression sickness.

task loading
Increasing the number of activities that a person is attempting to perform at the same time.

technical diving
Diving that takes place beyond the scope of sport diving. Technical dives

usually involve decompression stops, overhead environments, and specialized techniques and equipment.

time-to-fly
The time from the end of your last dive until your body is free of excess nitrogen and it is considered possible to fly in an airplane without undue risk of decompression sickness. Almost all dive computers will calculate this function and display the time-to-fly whenever the diver is topside.

Type I decompression sickness
Decompression sickness that results in pain-only symptoms. There is no neurological involvement in this type of incident.

Type II decompression sickness
Decompression sickness that produces neurological symptoms, such as vertigo, paralysis, numbness, tingling, or other serious symptoms.

trimix
A gas mixture that contains nitrogen, oxygen, and helium and is used in deep diving.

vestibular decompression sickness
Decompression sickness that affects the diver's sense of balance. This type of incident is considered quite serious.

About SDI and TDI

About TDI

TDI was formed in 1994 by some of diving's most experienced instructors to bring technical applications of the sport to a wider audience. TDI's library of training materials and texts have become known as the industry's best and most professional resources. Most importantly, TDI has the best safety record of all training agencies.

Whether your interests lie in nitrox, rebreathers, mixed gas or any of the many other programs that TDI offers, you can be assured that you will be participating in training that offers you the "cutting edge" of diving technology. With offices worldwide and over 10,000 instructors teaching our programs, TDI has become the largest international specialized dive agency.

About SDI

SDI grew out of the success of our sister company TDI, which specialized in more advanced disciplines of dive training. Our instructors asked for an entry level scuba training program that would reflect that same forward-looking approach that TDI brought to technical diving pursuits.

Finally after a year in development, the SDI training program was launched at the 1999 DEMA show. It was an instant success on its own merits. Both students and instructors have embraced the no nonsense approach that the SDI training system offers. We have streamlined the course materials to let students study the essential academics with a renewed emphasis on practical diving skills learned in both the pool and open water environments. SDI was the first to require students to be taught with modern dive computers from the outset.

Diving is constantly changing. Many other agencies are still mired in yesterday while our staff looks ahead to the millennium and strives to continue our record as the innovators of the industry. We want to make the experience of diving one that is enjoyed by every family member to the fullest. At SDI we are all divers and want to share our love of the sport with as wide an audience as possible. Please check out the variety of programs at SDI and join us in our passion!

SDI DIVER PROGRAMS

SCUBA DIVING INTERNATIONAL

Open Water Diver
▼
Advanced Diver Development Program
◄ **(4 Specialty Diver Courses)**
▼
Advanced Diver ► **Solo Diver**
▼
Rescue Diver ► **Divemaster**
▼   ▼
Master Diver Program   **Assistant Instructor**
◄ **(8 Specialty Diver Courses)**   ▼
Instructor ◄
▼
Instructor Trainer

- Altitude Diver
- Boat Diver
- Computer Diver
- Computer Nitrox Diver
- CPROX Administrator
- CPR1st Administrator
- Deep Diver (130ft Max)
- Diver Propulsion Vehicle
- Drift Diver
- Dry Suit Diver
- Equipment Specialist
- Ice Diver
- Marine Ecosystems Awareness
- Night/ Limited Visibility Diver
- Research Diver
- Search & Recovery Diver
- Shore/Beach Diver
- Underwater Navigation
- Underwater Photography
- Underwater Video
- Wreck Diver
- Underwater Hunter & Collector

About the Author
Steve Barsky

Steve Barsky started diving in 1965 in Los Angeles County, and became a diving instructor in 1970. His first employment in the industry was with a dive store in Los Angeles, and he went on to work for almost 10 years in the retail dive store environment.

Steve attended the University of California at Santa Barbara, where he earned a Masters Degree in 1976 in Human Factors/Ergonomics. This has helped greatly in his thorough understanding of diving equipment design and use. His master's thesis was one of the first to deal with the use of underwater video systems in commercial diving. His work was a pioneering effort at the time (1976) and was used by the Navy in developing applications for underwater video systems.

His background includes being a commercial diver, working in the offshore oil industry in the North Sea, Gulf of Mexico, and South America. He worked as both an air diving supervisor and a mixed gas saturation diver, making working dives down to 580'.

Barsky was marketing manager for Viking America, Inc., an international manufacturer of dry suits. He also served in a similar position at Diving Systems International (DSI), the world's leading manufacturer of commercial diving helmets.

Steve is an accomplished underwater photographer. His photos have been used in numerous magazine articles, catalogs, advertising, training programs, and textbooks.

A prolific writer, Barsky's work has been published in *Sea Technology, Skin Diver, Offshore Magazine, Emergency, Fire Engineering, Dive Training Magazine, Searchlines, Sources, Undersea Biomedical Reports, Santa Barbara Magazine, Underwater Magazine*, and many other publications. He is the author of the *Dry Suit Diving Manual, Diving in High Risk Environments, California Lobster Diving, Spearfishing for Skin and Scuba Divers, Small Boat Diving, Diving with the EXO-26 Full Face Mask, Diving with the Divator MK II Full Face Mask*, and a joint author with Dick Long and Bob Stinton of *Dry Suit Diving: A Guide to Diving Dry*. Steve has taught numerous workshops on contaminated water diving, dry suits, small boat diving, spearfishing, and other diving topics. *The Simple Guide to Rebreather Diving* was written by Steve along with Mark Thurlow and Mike Ward.

For Scuba Diving International, Steve has authored this book, as well as *Easy Nitrox Diving with Dive Computers. Night Diving, Underwater Navigation, and Limited Visibility Diving Techniques* is another title and *Wreck Diving and Boat Diving Techniques* is also available.

In 1989 Steve formed Marine Marketing and Consulting, based in Santa Barbara, California. The company provides market research, marketing plans, consulting, newsletters, promotional articles, technical manuals, and other services for the diving and ocean industry. He has consulted to Dräger, AquaLung/U.S. Divers Co., Inc, Zeagle Systems, Inc., Light and Motion, Diving Unlimited Intnl., Diving Systems Intnl, DAN, NAUI, and numerous other companies.

He also investigates diving accidents and serves as an expert witness in dive accident litigation.

In 1999, Steve and his wife Kristine formed Hammerhead Press to publish high quality diving books. Hammerhead Press is a subsidiary of the Carcharodon Corporation.

Steve is an instructor with SDI, TDI, and other certifying organizations. You can purchase Steve's other books at your local dive store, or on-line at http://www.hammerheadpress.com/

Index

Index

Index